The Bible Reader's Companion:

The Writings of Luke and John

New Testament Samples from <u>The Bible Reader's Companion</u>: Gospel of Luke, Acts of the Apostles, Gospel of John, I, II, III John, Revelation

Rob Swanson

First Edition (2017)

Copyright 2013, 2017 by Rob Swanson

Self Published with CreateSpace by Rob Swanson

Books > Religion and Spirituality > Christian Books and Bibles > Bible Study and Reference > Commentaries; Meditations

The Bible Reader's Companion, *Genesis-Revelation* is available through Amazon.com.

Rob Swanson
48 Henry F. Loring Rd.
Centerville, MA 02632
biblereaderscompanion@gmail.com

ISBN-13:**978-1540375377**
ISBN-10:**1540375374**

Table of Contents

Preface

It is presumptuous to think most Bible readers are involved in a study of the whole. Hence, the publication of New Testament samples include Luke and John. Old Testament samples from David and Solomon are also available.

The Bible Reader's Companion was written to help readers enjoy an engaging reading of the Bible. The writings of any particular author have a more limited range. But it is beneficial to delve into Bible segments for particular familiarity, to be followed with other studies within Genesis - Revelation, included in The Bible Reader's Companion, second edition.

Luke, the exemplary physician from Antioch according to tradition, became a pioneer missionary (Acts 16.10) and revelatory historian (Luke 1.3) through the ministry of the Holy Spirit.

John was an old man before he became a writer … and prophet! 90% of his gospel is unique. His letters reveal philosophy, theology and pastoral counsel. And Revelation is an apocalyptic expression not seen since Zechariah. No one saw this coming!

We thank God for the obedience and faithfulness of these two chosen instruments

Rob Swanson, September, 2016

Preface to The Bible Reader's Companion

The mind of God is complex and glorious and the Bible is as close as we can get to it. (Psalm 19.7-10; 2 Corinthians 4.4). This mind was revealed over millennia, with many literary styles, and to an audience contemporary and future.

The life of God is received and shaped by the Holy Spirit through the agency of written Scripture, God's gift (Daniel 2.22). Seeking the Lord begins with seeking a full understanding of his disclosed Word which was written carefully, by slow writers, for slow readers, and for the purpose of soul-formation.

With any single reading of the Bible much is missed. The number of angles and applications exceed the brain's capacity to process. So we happily keep at it, and for a lifetime. After a good reading comes study, then knowledge, and often personal illumination. Living out the Bible (obedience) follows the reading and reflection. But it starts with stimulating, delightful, interactive, engaging reading.

Read it, yes, but learn to turn the reading into dialog with God, life and self. Glean, apply and conform, in order to be transformed. Let the language of Scripture be the vocabulary of thoughts and conversation.

Bible knowledge is life sustaining, purpose giving and stress relieving. Most of all, it discloses knowledge of God and for his glory.

No part of the Bible is irrelevant—a fact that can be missed if the reading bogs down. Every iota and dot (Matthew 5.18) has been preserved as well as the phrases, sentences and paragraphs. The Bible Reader's Companion was written to further Bible exploration with over 2700 entries.

The Bible Reader's Companion lies in the seam between commentary and devotional. The benefit in Bible reading is in observation, appreciation, and personal application. Toward that end, may The Bible Reader's Companion be an aid. Writing and re-writing The Bible Reader's Companion was a joy with personal benefit to the author beyond any for the reader. No entry is dull as no section of the Bible is dull. No entry was written with strain. Surprisingly, *all* were fresh.

Digest the Bible (Matthew 4.4). Delight in it (Psalm 1.2).

Get acquainted with the sacred writings (2 Timothy 3.15).

Abide in the Bible and overcome the evil one (1 John 2.13).

Honorable mention goes to F.B. Meyer's Commentary, an appreciated classic for 20th century Bible readers. The Bible Reader's Companion follows in that honored tradition. Thanks to Crossway for permission to use their English Standard Version. It is those words The Bible Reader's Companion wishes to implant (James 1.27). Thanks to Phil Weingart, my wise and publication experienced friend and author for his invaluable work in this project.

Notes:

Psalm 19.7-10 The law of the Lord is perfect, reviving the soul;

the testimony of the Lord is sure, making wise the simple;
the precepts of the Lord are right, rejoicing the heart;
the commandment of the Lord is pure, enlightening the eyes;
the fear of the Lord is clean, enduring forever;
the rules of the Lord are true, and righteous altogether.
More to be desired are they than gold, even much fine gold;
sweeter also than honey and drippings of the honeycomb.

2 Corinthians 4.6 *For God, who said, "Let light shine out of darkness," has shone in our hearts to give the light of the knowledge of the glory of God in the face of Jesus Christ.*

Daniel 2.22 *he reveals deep and hidden things; he knows what is in the darkness, and the light dwells with him.*

Matthew 4.4 *But he answered, "It is written, "Man shall not live by bread alone, but by every word that comes from the mouth of God.""*

Psalm 1.2 *but his delight is in the law of the Lord, and on his law he meditates day and night.*

2 Timothy 3.15 *and how from childhood you have been acquainted with the sacred writings, which are able to make you wise for salvation through faith in Christ Jesus.*

Matthew 5.18 *For truly, I say to you, until heaven and earth pass away, not an iota, not a dot, will pass from the Law until all is accomplished.*

1 John 2.13 *I am writing to you, young men, because you have overcome the evil one.*

James 1.21 Therefore put away all filthiness and rampant wickedness and receive with meekness the implanted word, which is able to save your souls.

Rob Swanson, September, 2016

Introduction to The Bible Reader's Companion, First Edition

The purpose of <u>The Bible Reader's Companion</u> is to help readers **receive with meekness the implanted word** (James 1.21). It is observation driven, many of which stand without comment. The reader will hopefully be stimulated to add many more insights with personal applications—a normal blessing attendant to Bible reading.

<u>The Bible Reader's Companion</u> is to be read along with the Bible and other study aids. Most verses are quoted only in part. Entries are short and to be read without hurry, along with the cross-references.

As the Bible's literary style varies from book to book, so does the writing style in this volume. Some entries are short and clippy *or* muse over a few words *or* run on, tracking the progression of a lengthy section. Little effort is given to ferret out deeper meanings.

Sometimes a love for God sends me to the Word. More often, and after reading through the Bible annually for 36 years, it is the wisdom, nurture, guidance and vitality of God's revelation that draws me to him!

<u>The Bible Reader's Companion</u> was a joy to write! My thanks to Clara who provided motivation promising, *Grampa, if you write a book, I will read it.*

The ESV Study Bible (The English Standard Version) is a most excellent work and invaluable contribution to this generation. The Bible Reader's Companion hopes to be a compliment and bless you in your next round of reading and appreciating Genesis through Revelation or portions thereof. We all must read the Bible but need not read it alone!

Rob Swanson, November 4, 2013

Come, Holy Ghost (for moved by thee
The prophets wrote and spoke)
Unlock the truth, thyself the key,
Unseal the sacred book.

– *Charles Wesley*

LUKE

Luke

Even though **many have undertaken to compile a narrative** (Luke 1.1), Luke was undeterred and wrote his own **orderly account** (v. 3), for which the world is grateful. Faith needs information (v. 4). Why not him as he had **followed all things closely for some time** (v. 3)? His primary resources were not just **eyewitnesses** (v. 2) but faithful eyewitnesses, **ministers of the Word** (v. 2), thus disclosing a principle: credibility is a function of knowledge *and* acts of service.

many have undertaken to compile a narrative (Luke 1.1)– not just Matthew, Mark, Josephus, Q(?). **eyewitnesses … believers in the word** (v. 2) understandably sought a written record of their experiences and **things that have been accomplished** (v. 2). Luke, **having followed all things closely for some time … write**(s) **an orderly account** (v. 3) beginning with **Zechariah** … (and) **Elizabeth** (v. 5) and ending with Paul's imprisonment in Rome (Acts 28.30).

Zechariah: **on duty, according to the custom of the priesthood … burn**(ing) **incense** (Luke 1.8). **serving as a priest** (v. 8) was symbolic–dull, but purposeful! Being **righteous before God, walking blamelessly** (v. 6), **there appeared to him an angel of the Lord** (v. 11) announcing **your prayer has been heard** (v. 13)–a prayer either about (1) **Elizabeth** (who) **was barren** (v. 7) or (2) his **desire to turn many of the children of Israel to the Lord their God** (v. 16). Even beyond this, it was the dawn of a new era!

the custom of the priesthood (Luke 1.9) is not chided as superfluous legalism (v. 10), rather it is the context for angelic visitation. **righteous and blameless** Zechariah (v. 6) apparently was troubled over having no children (v. 13). He responds to Gabriel with **fear** (v. 12) and lengthy argument (vv. 18, 21), for which he will pay (v. 22). More importantly, he **will have joy and gladness** (v. 14) with a son **filled with the Holy Spirit ... in the spirit and power of Elijah** (vv. 15, 17), fulfilling Malachi 3.1!

Elizabeth, though **righteous** (Luke 1.6) suffered, receiving **reproach among people** (v. 25) for her **barren**(ness) (v. 36). The angel announces **joy and gladness** (v. 14) = God cares for his daughter ... daughters: **Mary** ... (having) **found favor with God** (vv. 27, 30), is promised **the power of the Most High will overshadow you** (v. 35). **Mary arose and went haste** ... (to) **the house of Zechariah** (vv. 39, 40) and is affirmed by Elizabeth and **the baby ... in her womb** (v. 41; cf. vv. 41-45). Pro-choice sympathizers, take note.

Mary's encounter with Gabriel 5 months later focuses on the dialog, not the context. She understands he is announcing Messiah (Luke 1.32, 33). **He will be great** (v. 32). She does not understand a virgin birth, but knows what she heard and responds, **nothing is impossible with God ... let it be to me according to your word** (vv. 37, 38). Gabriel's introduction of Jesus and Mary's description of humble obedience (vv. 30-38) are oft quoted and remembered for all time.

Mary **magnifies the Lord** (Luke 1.46). He is **Savior ... mighty** (vv. 47, 49). **And his mercy is for those who fear him** (v. 50), emphasized again in vv. 54, 58, 72, 78. Is any key to life more central? Mary *got it!*–happy with her **humble estate** (vv. 48, 52). All of this is nothing new. **He has shown strength ...fill**(ing) **the hungry with good things** (vv. 51, 53). Conversely, **the proud ... the mighty ... the rich** (vv. 51-53), i.e. the godless, receive his opposition (vv. 51-53).

Mary's song (Luke 1.46-55) reveals a Luke distinctive: *God's kingdom values oppose and conquer the norms of the world.* The humble are **blessed** (v. 48). The proud are **scattered** (v. 51). God does great things for the humble and for his **holy ... name** (vv. 49-51). He brings down **the mighty** (v. 52). Mary is filled with praise (vv. 46, 47) and with thoughts of God's **mercy** (vv. 50, 54). These expressions of God's will are resisted by the world while bringing delight to the saved.

Zechariah, like Elizabeth and John, is **filled with the Holy Spirit** (Luke 1.15, 41). His prophecy (vv. 67-79) is an informative picture of Messiah. (1) The final victory: **that we should be saved from our enemies and from the hand of all who hate us** (v. 71; also vv. 69, 74). (2) The means: Messiah would **give knowledge of salvation ... in the forgiveness of sins ... give light ... guide into the way of peace** (vv. 77, 79). Missing for now: the suffering on the cross and the winning of nations.

Zechariah and Elizabeth receive pressure from **neighbors and relatives** (Luke 1.58) **to call** (their baby) **Zechariah after his father, but His mother answered, "No ..."** (vv. 59, 60) and Zechariah **wrote, His name is John** (v. 63). They submit to the revelation (v. 13) over custom. People of faith are radical! **Zechariah ... prophesied ... serve him without fear, in holiness and righteousness ... all our days. And you child ...**

prophet of the Most High ... will go before the Lord to prepare his ways, to give knowledge of salvation (vv. 67-77).

And all went to be registered, each to his own town (Luke 2.3). What a pain! 90 miles of travel and weeks of unemployment for a silly, unnecessary administrative matter. Or, what an excitement! Mary was likely now even more familiar with prophecy than when she recited Luke 1.46-55. If so, she knew about Micah 5.2. God had arranged Jesus' birth in the village of Messiah! No one anticipated **a manger** (v. 12). The Son of God was humble (see Philippians 2.7) from the start.

God's method of operation is on display in Luke 2.1-15: (1) Arduous obligations are not treated as burdens. The **decree ... that all the world should be registered** (v. 1) was an onerous proclamation. **Joseph ...** (traveling) **from Galilee ... to ... Bethlehem ... with Mary, his betrothed** (vv. 4, 5), is similarly recorded without comment. **She gave birth** (v. 7) is all we know about labor and delivery. (2) Life includes infrequent but grand interventions. **An angel of the Lord appeared to ... shepherds** (vv. 9, 8) for the purpose of recognition, lest *stones cry out (19.40)!*

When God does a work, joyful praise is expected now as it was then. So it was at the incarnation. There was no shortage of excitement for those in the know! The angel announced **good news of a great joy** (Luke 2.10). **A multitude of heavenly hosts** (were) **praising God** (v. 13). the shepherds (were) **glorifying and praising God** (v. 20). **Simeon ... blessed God** (vv. 25, 28). **his father and mother marveled** (v. 33).

Mary had much to **treasure ... in her heart** (vv. 19, 51). Indeed!

The shepherds and Simeon received revelation concerning **a Savior, who is Christ ... the Lord's Christ** (Luke 2.11, 26). The shepherds **went with haste ... to Bethlehem ... by night** (vv. 16, 15, 8) and **returned, glorifying and praising God** (Luke 2.20), just as **the heavenly host** (was) **praising God and saying, "Glory to God in the highest ...** (v. 14). Simeon ... **righteous and devout ... came in the Spirit into the temple ... took (the child) up in his arms** (v. 25, 27, 28) and prophesied **glory to ... Israel** (v. 32; see vv. 29-32).

Senior citizens play a major role in the Christmas account: **Zechariah, Elizabeth, Anna** and presumable **Simeon** (Luke 1.5-25, 39-45, 57-80; 2.25-38). God honored their **walking blameless in all the commandments and statutes ... worshiping with fasting day and night** (1.6, 2.37). Upon such God gave a spirit of prophecy. They lived in tough times. Most years were disappointing. Or were they? Living in God's presence brings purpose, joy and vigor. To the faithful God reveals and provides.

Each witness to the incarnation–the angels, shepherds, parents of John and Jesus–has something to add. Simeon saw in Jesus **a light for revelation to the Gentiles** (Luke 2.32) and **the fall and rising of many in Israel** (v. 34). The good news also incites enmity. Like Simeon, Anna lived her long life in a spiritual zone (vv. 25, 37). She intuitively knew the baby Jesus was for the long awaited **redemption of Jerusalem** (v. 38) and effusively **began to give thanks to God and to speak of him** (v. 38).

Likely through the testimony of Mary, Luke sheds light on Jesus' childhood. The family lived **according to custom** (Luke 2.42). Jesus was not considered solitary, rather at home **in the group** (v. 44) and in religious discussions (vv. 46, 47, 49). Jesus was venturesome–**three days** (v. 46) on his own, yet **was submissive to** (v. 51) his parents. Though divine, he was ever increas(ing) **in wisdom and … in favor with God and man** (v. 52).

Keeping with his writing objectives (Luke 1.1-4), Luke identifies 7 contemporary leaders at the time **the word of God came to John** (3.2). Such a spiritual experience was not for private consumption. **He went into all the region … proclaiming a baptism of repentance** (3.3), so as to **Prepare the way of the Lord** (3.4; Isaiah 40.3-50). Bold! One man confronting the world! Confrontational: **to the crowds … You brood of vipers … even now the axe is laid to the root of the trees** (3.7, 9)! All part of the **good news** (v. 18)!

John's preaching is more challenging than it is condemning. hav(ing) **Abraham as our father** (Luke 3.8) is of no benefit without **Bear(ing) fruits keeping with repentance** (v. 8); shar(ing) **tunics** (and) … **food** (v. 11). Among the respondents, **Tax collectors … Soldiers** (vv. 12, 14)! **the people were in expectation** (v. 15)! John is quick to deflect attention to **he who is mightier** (and who) **is coming** (v. 16), whose message will be far more severe (v. 17). **Herod,** sensitive to the criticism, **locked up John in prison** (vv. 19, 20).

John, a notable personality of the day, and certainly of chapter 3, was **the voice crying in the wilderness** (v. 4; cf.

Isaiah 40.3). Many hoped **he might be the Christ** (v. 15). He was loved for his **good news** (v. 18) despite lacing his message with condemnation (vv. 7-9). John prepared people for even harsher words coming from Jesus (v. 17). Luke authenticates his research with name-dropping–the people who set the historical context, from Jesus' genealogy (Luke 3.23-38) to the contemporary leaders (vv. 1, 2).

when … he was praying, the heavens were opened and the Holy Spirit descended (Luke 3.21, 22). Divine activity follows prayer, even for the **beloved Son** (3.22). The **Son** reference prompts Luke to include the genealogy (3.23-38). **full of the Holy Spirit … and … led by the Spirit** … (Jesus travels to) **the wilderness for forty days** (4.1, 2). What?! Hunger, austerity, temptation–it does not sound good. It *is* an example of divine leading and providence and for Jesus, a prelude to even greater **power** (4.14).

In tempting Jesus, Satan opens with his best shot. Temptation #1: **If you are the Son of God, command this stone to become bread** (Luke 4.3). He strikes at Jesus' identity / his character! And then requests such a simple sign, all with Jesus in a weaken state. Luther in *A Might Fortress* … got it right: "one little word shall fell him," especially when that word is from written Scripture (see vv. 4, 8, 12). Failing here, I give Satan no chance as he tempts Jesus with acquisitions and notoriety (vv. 6, 7, 10, 11).

Luke 4.7-30 is *all religion*. Temptation #2 is an attempt to divert **worship** *from* the living God and *to* Satan (Luke 4.7). In temptation #3 Satan demonstrates his cleverness at *Scripture speak* (vv. 10, 11; Psalm 91. 11, 12). **Jesus returned**

... to Galilee ... (and) **taught in their synagogues** (vv. 14, 15). The topic: his identity and the value system of the kingdom of God (vv. 18, 19). Jesus' interpretation of Elijah's **legacy filled with wrath ... all in the synagogue** (v. 20, 28). Threatened with violence (v. 29), **he went away** (v. 30)!

Jesus was introduced as **the son of God** (Luke 3.38) and *that* claim was contested by the **devil** (4.3). Turning stones to bread: a "no win" proposal. = *Jesus, do as I say or you are not the Son of God.* Jesus quotes the word of God, smashing the temptation. Was Jesus supposed to receive a kingdom offered by the devil (4.6, 7)? Ridiculous! **put the Lord ... to the test** (4.12) at the devil's initiative? We do *nothing* at his suggestion! Be gone! And he was **until** ... (another) **opportune time** (4.13).

Like John, Jesus was loved—**being glorified by all** (Luke 4.14). Unlike John, he was hated: **all in the synagogue were filled with wrath** (v. 28). For this all Jesus had to do was turn the subject matter *to himself* (vv. 18, 19). People with large egos are threatened by greater personalities (e.g. **Elijah ... Elisha**– vv. 26, 27). Jesus was not **acceptable in his hometown** (v. 24). The One worthy of praise is rebuffed!

The deserved praise and acknowledgment would not be denied. **you are–the Holy One of God** (Luke 4.34) comes from **an unclean demon** (v. 33), and demons knew he was the Christ (v. 34)! **And reports about him went out into every place** (v. 37). Through healing and preaching, Israel is exposed to the presence of Messiah (vv. 38-43) and a new understanding of **the kingdom of God** (v. 43).

Luke 5 & 6 showcase the life, times and teachings of Jesus more than any other section of similar length. 5.1-11 models the unpredictable flow of ministry: Teaching a crowd **the word of God** (5.1), then teaching from a boat, then the challenge to cast out the nets, then Peter's conviction and call to catch men, then **they left everything** (v. 11). What a memorable time! Jesus always *attracts and impresses,* followed by *calling and commissioning* those well aware of their unworthiness (v. 8).

all … were astonished (Luke 5.9): a fitting banner for the disparate narrative of Luke 4.31-5.11. (1) Jesus is known for his **teaching** (4.31; cf. vv. 36, 44; 5.1, 3). **I was sent for this purpose** (4.43). The miraculous catch of **a large number of fish** (5.6) serves to illustrate a teaching (5.10). (2) Like **the devil** (4.2), demons have no doubt about Jesus' identity (**Son of God** – 4.3, 41) and intentions: **you come to destroy us … they knew that he was the Christ** (4.34, 31). (3) Healings accompany the exorcisms (4.39, 40) through **rebuke** (4.39) and **la**(ying) **his hands on them** (4.40), the victims.

Peter was called to **catch … men** (Luke 5.10). The healed leper was **charged … to tell no one** (v. 14). Like Jesus, Luke is not concerned about confusing us. He is concerned that we, like **the priest** (v. 14), become convinced that Jesus is the Messiah. Jesus demonstrates love and power. As **the report about him went abroad** (v. 15), **he would withdraw to desolate places and pray** (v. 16, cf. 6.12)–no small observations! Jesus discloses the kingdom of God and models doing it.

great crowds gathered to hear him and to be healed (Luke 5.15). Jesus mission was to teach and show mercy … and lay low–**tell no one … he would withdraw to desolate places** (vv. 14, 16). He combined healing and teaching to **a man who was paralyzed** (v. 18) and the surrounding **scribes and Pharisees** (v. 20): **Rise and walk … the Son of Man has authority on earth to forgive sins** (vv. 23, 24). The response was **amazement … question**(ing) … **grumbl**(ing) (vv. 26, 21, 30).

Jesus had a following of Pharisees (Luke 5.17, 30, 33; 6.2, 7). They **had come from every village of Galilee and Judea and from Jerusalem** (5.17). Jesus was the main attraction (6.17). After healing the paralytic, they were impressed. **We have seen extraordinary things today** (5.26). But Jesus had not come for them (5.32). In fact he likened them to **old wineskins** (5.37) for which he was a poor match (5.36-39). Early praise morphs into accusation and rejection (6.2, 7).

As Jesus demonstrates his mastery of the word of God, established beliefs are exposed resulting in opposition and conflict. Eating **some heads of grain** (Luke 6.1) and **heal**(ing) **on the Sabbath** (vv. 6, 10) were quite appropriate but represented a new teaching–something different–change. As **power came out of him** (v. 20), **they were filled with fury** (v. 11). Certain Pharisees were blind and wanted to *get him* (v. 11). Jesus polarizes.

By now it is evident that Jesus is the offset to the fallenness all around him. He is putting the right side up! He is life in living color against the black and white sinful world. The healings are undeniable. Next up: teachings–the sermon **on a** level place (Luke 6.17). The poor, hungry and weeping are not really at a disadvantage to those who are **rich ... full ...** (and) **laugh** (vv. 20-26). **enemies** are to be loved (v. 27). Gifts need not be returned or compensated in other ways (vv. 30-36). **forgive** (v. 37)! You got to love this!

he lifted his eyes up on his disciples (Luke 6.20) to present the sermon **on a level place** (v. 17)–vv. 20-49. Why is there a blessing for **you who are poor ... hungry ... weep now ... and spurn**(ed etc.) **... on account of the Son of Man** (vv. 21, 22)? All who stand with **the prophets ...** (shall) **laugh ... leap with joy** (vv. 23, 21). The scales of eternity favor the person who rejects faulty world standards and lives by truth (vv. 46-49), with a **foundation on the rock** (v. 48).

Luke 6.27-45, part 2 of the sermon **on a level place** (v. 17), is a discourse on self-effacing love. Specifically, **love your enemies ... those who hate you ...** (the) **one who strikes you on the cheek ...** (the) **one who takes away** (vv. 27-30), etc. Remember, **your reward will be great** (v. 35)–once again, Jesus measuring life according to eternity. Elsewhere, I read about the Holy Spirit's role in personal transformation (e.g. Romans 8). Here, Jesus presents the goal: **Be merciful ... Judge not ... give ... take the log out of your own eye** (vv. 36-38).

Love your enemies, do good to those who hate you, bless those who persecute you, pray for those who abuse you. To the one who strikes you on the cheek, offer the other ... Give (Luke 6.27-30). Every Christian and at every stage of maturity is challenged here ... and humbled! I am reminded to de-value my standing in this world as I value the kingdom of God. Jesus: **blessed is the one who is not offended by me** (7.23).

More on the alternative world of Jesus: Luke 6.39-49 describes the real losers in his kingdom four ways: They are (1) **blind** and unable to lead (v. 39); (2) harsh on others and accepting of self (vv. 39-42); (3) producing bad fruit from **the abundance of the heart** (v. 45); (4) religious but not obedient: **you call me 'Lord, Lord,' and do not do what I tell you** (v. 46). **hypocrite**(s) (v. 42) receive a falling (v. 39) and **ruin** (v. 49).

So it goes for those who exalt and defend *their* way. Contrast the blind and hypocrite (Luke 6.39, 42) with: (1) the **centurion** of Capernaum (7.1-10), a man who loved his **servant** (!) and Israel (!) and saw his own insignificance compared to Jesus (7.2, 5, 6); (2) the crowd around the **widow** of Nain (7.11-17). **They glorified God, saying, "A great prophet has arisen amongst us!"** (7.16). God continues to provide ways to acknowledge the Messiah.

Jesus condemns the **hypocrite** (Luke 6.42), **the evil person** (6.45) and **the man who built his house on the ground without a foundation** (6.49). He is citing character / heart issues ahead of deeds. The same is true for (1) the **centurion** (7.2)–grace for one *not* **poor … hungry** (6.20, 21). Whew! (2) Death had been accepted and there were no requests on behalf of **a man who had died** (and) **was being carried out** (7.12). Then with his **compassion** (7.13) stirred, Jesus responds to **faith** (7.9).

Jesus addresses **Pharisees and teachers of the law** (Luke 7.17) in chapters 5 & 6 (5.30, 33; 6.2, 7, 24-26, 39, 43, 46). Conflict gives rise to the teaching opportunities for memorable learning. So, good arises from difficulty and opposition—a life principle. These great teachings include, **I have not come to call the righteous, but sinners ... new wine must be put into fresh wineskins ... The Son of Man is lord of the Sabbath** (5.32; 5.38; 6.5).

The perspective of Jesus on life and circumstances is radical and often contrary to common sense. (1) Jesus consents to John's imprisonment. John is not happy about it and inquires why (Luke 7.18-20). Before responding, Jesus continues serving, **he healed many** (v. 21), and he wants the report of that to satisfy his suffering second cousin. Then he gives John the highest of accolades (v. 28). He announces **the least in the kingdom of God is greater** (v. 28). Why? Imputed righteousness (see 1 Corinthians 1.30).

John would have appreciated a little acknowledgement as he sat and suffered in prison (Luke 7.18-30). As far as he could tell, nothing was happening. Jesus does not come to his aid. **blessed is the one who is not offended** (v. 23). Jesus commends John, as there are none **in the kingdom of God ... greater than he** (v. 28). Jesus goes on fulfilling the greater **purpose of God** (v. 30), healing, and bestowing light (v. 21), figuratively and literally!

the people of this generation ... what are they like? (Luke 7.21). Hard to please! They want to select the tunes for the real leaders to **dance** (7.32). Jesus told **the Pharisees** (who) **asked to eat with him ... you gave me no water for my feet**

... You gave me no kiss ... You did not anoint my head (7.36, 44-46) = no heart ... no affection. They take **the word of God** (8.11) and **trample** (it) **underfoot** (8.5), or **give it no root** (8.13), or **go on their way** (to be) **choked by the cares and riches and pleasures of life** (8.14). Thank God for the exceptions (7.37; 8.2, 8)!

Noticeably absent so far is the doctrine of the cross, which will be introduced in Luke 9.22. For now, the presentation is of kingdom living and the challenges of faith: **Your faith has saved you ... Where is your faith? ... Your faith has made you well ... only believe** (Luke 7.50; 8.25, 48, 50). Spiritual life begins with and is through faith. Until death I am in the school of faith, i.e. I am learning to understand and trust the person and purposes of the living God.

Women have a major role in Jesus' ministry, then and now: (1) The **woman of the city** (Luke 7.37) models worship–expressive and lavish (7.36-38). She shows love and receives forgiveness (7.47, 48). (2) Jesus and the twelve **went on through the cities and villages** (8.1) with 3 women **and many others, who provided for them out of their means** (8.3). (3) Then there was the woman of faith who fought the crowds **falling down before him declared in the presence of all why she had touched him** 8.47). Bold!

Life hinges on how well I handle **the word of God** (Luke 8.11). I must give it **root ... hold it fast** (vv. 13, 15). **thorns ... cares and riches and pleasures of life** (v. 14) will **choke** it. **bear fruit with patience** (v. 15). **hear the word of God and do it** (v. 20). **to the one who has, more will be given** (v. 18). **hear** (5x in vv. 10-21) = understand. Soon after, **his disciples** heard

Jesus **rebuke ... a windstorm** (vv. 22-24)–authority to match the teaching!

As with Luke 5.1-11, 8.22-39 presents the unpredictable, spontaneous and serendipitous nature of Christian life and Christian ministry. (Nothing against planning and routines!) Jesus **sail**(s) **to the country of the Gerasenes** (Luke 8.26) and along the way the disciples learn something about the Jesus' power and identity. Jesus sleeps through, and then calms **a windstorm** (8.22-25). He heals a man **who had demons** (8.26-33). More excitement on the return trip ...

Jairus (Luke 8.41), like the **centurion** (7.2), was a man of social standing who sought Jesus because his heart was breaking. The immanence of death and loss tend to do that! **falling at Jesus' feet he implored him** (8.41). Good move! When Jesus instructed, **only believe** (8.50), I assume he did! May all of us present such a demeanor to God! Jesus then brings a girl back from the dead for the joy of it and certainly not to further his reputation. **tell no one** (8.56).

In contrast to the derision and challenges he received from Pharisees (Luke 5-7), Jesus is now receiving worthy recognition. His disciples marveled, **Who then is this?** (8.25). The **man from the city who had demons ... fell down before him** (vv. 27, 28) and later was **sitting at the feet of Jesus ...** (and) **begged that he might be with him** (vv. 35, 38). **the herdsmen ...** (and) **all the people from the surrounding country ... were seized with great fear** (vv. 34, 37). Then **the** crowd welcomed him ... (including) **a ruler of the synagogue** (vv. 40, 41)!

I perceive that power has gone out of me (Luke 8.46). Some prayers are responded to immediately. See John 14.12-14; 16.24. Jesus stopped to have this hidden ... woman who had a discharge of blood for twelve years (vv. 47, 43) tell her story to the people pressed around him (vv. 42) = more worthy recognition. (See 8.25-41.) Similarly, those who were weeping and mourning ... (and) laughed at him (vv. 52, 53) would give honorable recognition once he raised the little girl from the dead (v. 53)!

Jesus overwhelms his followers: (1) He gives them power and authority ... and sen(ds) them out to proclaim ... and heal (Luke 9.1, 2). (2) Fresh opposition from Herod the tetrarch (vv. 7-9). Intimidating! (3) He tells the 12 to feed 5,000. They claim limited resources, so Jesus does it himself (vv. 37-43)! (4) Jesus prophesies tough times–his suffering, rejection, execution, and on the third day be raised (v. 22). (5) If anyone would come after me, let him deny himself and take up his cross (v. 23).

Jesus wants his disciples to share his experiences. So, he gave them power and authority over all demons and to cure diseases, and he sent them out to proclaim ... and heal (Luke 9.1, 2), and with few provisions (v. 3). They went ... preaching the gospel and healing everywhere (v. 6) and presumably, like him, receiving rejection (v. 5). All of this is tiring. When they withdrew, Jesus still welcomed ... the crowds (v. 11). the twelve (:) ... send the crowd away (v. 12)!

More work: You give them something to eat (Luke 9.13). Each disciple was given about 8 groups of fifty (v. 15)! he broke the loaves and gave them to the disciples (v. 16) =

disciples–tired disciples–do the work with Jesus providing. A timeless principle. **left over**(s)–another such principle! In due time came rest, prayer and reflection where they talk about Jesus identity (vv. 18-20), **John the Baptist** (v. 19; cf. vv. 7-9), and new information: he would **be killed, and on the third day be raised** (v. 22).

The Son of Man must suffer ... (and a disciple) **take up his cross daily ... forfeit himself** (Luke 9.22, 23, 25). This *higher intensity* level in Jesus' teaching is followed by the transfiguration (vv. 28-36) with Jesus' **face ... altered, and his clothing dazzling white. And behold, two men talking with him, Moses and Elijah** (vv. 29, 30). The lesson from all this: Christo-centricity! Peter's confession (v. 20) is confirmed. **This is my Son, my Chosen One, listen to him!** (v. 35). Jesus–my salvation and wisdom.

Luke 9.23-36 directs attention to the future. Think *glory!* (1) Denying oneself, losing one's life, taking up a cross and following Jesus, are all commended **when he comes in his glory** (Luke 9.26). (2) **glory** surrounds Jesus at his transfiguration (v. 32). Note the context of prayer (vv. 18, 28). In both of these sections Jesus is exalted. God is manifested when the confirming voice does and does not come **out of the cloud** (v. 35).

Jesus is dealing with his disciples, demons and the imminence of his death (Luke 9.37-50). His disciples, riding high on recent miracles (vv. 6, 17, 29), try to cast out a demon **but they could not** (v. 40). So Jesus **rebuked the unclean spirit and healed the boy** (v. 42). He then asks the 12 to let his **words** (about **deliver**(ance) **into the hands of men -**

v. 44; cf. v. 22) **sink into their ears** (v. 44), to no avail amidst their sense of self-importance (v. 46). He points them to servitude–receiving **a child** (v. 47).

For the fourth time since 5.17, Jesus heals at the request on another (Luke 9.37-43). Jesus calls for faith (v. 41), demonstrates power (v. 42), **and all were astonished at the majesty of God** (v. 43). This demonstration of his greatness though is not enough to generate a corresponding humility in the 12. Quite to the contrary! **An argument arose ... as to which of them was the greatest** (v. 46). They even wanted to shut down an exorcist **because he does not follow with us** (v. 49).

Jesus and the world around him head in opposite directions. Always! The Samaritans want nothing to do with one whose **face was set toward Jerusalem** (Luke 9.53). Generations-old prejudice. Jesus wants little to do with (1) the offended, like James and John who wanted **fire to come down from heaven and consume them** (v. 55). Or, (2) those who placed their security on matters (vv. 57-62) other than issue #1: being **fit for the kingdom of God** (v. 62).

For the moment, Jesus has **Jerusalem** on his mind, not **Samari**(a) (Luke 9.51, 52). **Follow me** (9.59) was an invitation to his passion and his own burial! Jesus' focus, **the kingdom of God** (9.60, 62; 10.9, 11), begs to be **proclaim**(ed - 9.60). He **appointed seventy-two** (10.1) to do just that. **in the midst of wolves** (10.3) they would receive hospitality (10.7) and **Heal** (10.9) and warn (10.12-16), which compliments the other part of his message–**peace** (10.6).

Jesus never turns inward, even en route to Calvary. He **appointed seventy-two others and sent them on ahead** (Luke 10.1) with instructions (vv. 2-12). They can expect meeting **wolves** (v. 3) and **a son of peace** (v. 6). Hospitality distinguishes the two. In return, one receives healing and affirmation (v. 9), the other nothing. Those *rejecters* are identified with **all who shall be brought down to Hades** (v. 15). Rejecting a Christian witness = rejecting the Father (v. 16)!

Mission results in joy. **The seventy-two returned with joy** (Luke 10.17). Jesus **rejoiced** (v. 21). The Holy Spirit was sharing in that joy (v. 21)! Jesus added, **rejoice that your names are written in heaven** (v. 20). Lessons: (1) It should never be a surprise to see God work when I step outside my comfort zone on Jesus' behalf. (2) Mission attracts the fullness of God (who is full of joy). See Psalm 16.11. When lacking joy, get moving!

Blessed are the eyes that see what you see … and … hear what you hear (Luke 10.23, 24). And what was that? Essentially, a glimpse into the eternal state. (1) These socially inconsequential **little children** (v. 21) had **authority to tread on serpents and scorpions, and over all the power of the enemy** (v. 19; cf. Matthew 23.33). Believe it! (2) They heard Jesus **rejoice … I thank you Father** (v. 21) and go on to reveal the unique Father-Son relationship (v. 22). Such matters overshadow the trials of life.

The stories about **a lawyer** (Luke 10.25) and **a woman named Martha** (v. 38) share in common the shortcomings of self-reliance / self-focus. The lawyer was quite willing to match wits with Jesus, noting his knowledge and virtue (vv. 25-29). Jesus humbles him and sends him off–**You go** (v. 37). The **much serving** (v. 40) Martha was seen rather as **distracted ... anxious and troubled** (vv. 40, 41). Luke provides a contrast in the caring **Samaritan** (v. 33) and relational **Mary** (v. 39).

Jesus told the lawyer he already had the answer to his question about eternal life. It was *in the Law* and it concerned **love** (Luke 10.27). The lawyer's follow up question was not about love but **who is my neighbor?** (v. 29). Jesus does not give an academic answer but addresses the real need. "You be a neighbor!" Similarly with the question from Martha, **do you not care that my sister has left me to serve alone?** (v. 40). The real issue was her anxiety (v. 41), not unfairness. Her need at this time was to be more like Mary!

one of his disciples ... (wanted to learn prayer) **as John taught his disciples** (Luke 11.1). Jesus affirms (1) natural prayer–**Give us each day our daily bread** (v. 3); (2) heart prayer–**Father, hallowed be your name** (v. 2); (3) kingdom prayer–**Your kingdom come ... forgive us ... we ourselves forgive** (v. 3). Prayers that support kingdom principles are answered, e.g. **the Father give**(s) **the Holy Spirit to those who ask him!** (v. 13). (4) **impudence** (v. 8) = prayer need not be proper and polished.

Upon request, Jesus teaches prayer (Luke 11.2-4) and in two parts: (1) He models a kingdom centered prayer with the focus on *salvation* (**forgive us our sins**) and *integrity* (**hallowed be your name ... we ourselves forgive everyone ... lead us not into temptation**). (2) Jesus elevates the importance of petitioning. Sometimes it is like going to a friend **at**

midnight requesting bread to feed a traveller (vv. 5-8). God welcomes such requests much more than we would think. He has **good gifts for ...** (his) **children ...** (and) **the Holy Spirit to those who ask him** (v. 13)!

the people marveled. But some (Luke 11.14,15). This latter group thought, or expressed derision (crediting **Beelzebub,** v. 15) and dissatisfaction (they **kept seeking from him a sign –** v. 16). Addressing their ignorance, Jesus reveals truth about **demons** (vv. 17-26). He credits exorcising power to himself, the **strong man** (v. 21). It is the **finger of God ...** (manifesting) **the kingdom of God** (v. 20). Nonetheless, demons are a perilous force (v. 26), passing **through waterless places seeking rest** (v. 24).

More on Jesus' kingdom: **it is by the finger of God that I cast out demons** (Luke 11.20). With ease **the strong man** (v. 21) conquers the **divided household** of Satan (v. 17, cf. vv. 18, 21, 22). Demons remain a menace (vv. 24-26). Jesus' kingdom is **hear**(ing) **the word of God and keep**(ing) **it** (v. 28). It is recognizing **something greater than Solomon ... greater than Jonah** (vv. 31, 32). It is receiving and disclosing God's light (vv. 33-36; 12.35, 36). Jesus is the center of this revolutionary paradigm!

Luke 11.14-15.30 records Jesus' teaching to **people** (who) **marveled ... a woman in the crowd ... the crowds ... a Pharisee ... One of the lawyers ... the scribes and the Pharisees ... many thousands ... Someone in the crowd ... to the crowds ... some present at that very time ... in one of the synagogues ... someone ... some Pharisees ... the house of a ruler of the Pharisees ... great crowds ... tax collectors and sinners (11.14, 27, 29, 37, 53; 12.1, 13, 54; 13.1, 23, 31; 14.1, 25; 15.1). He does not hold back!

Jesus calls **This generation … an evil generation** (Luke 11.29) after rebuffing a compliment for his mother (v. 28). He indicts the whole generation, not the demonic (vv. 14-26), and those in power (vv. 37, 45, 53). **It seeks for a sign** (v. 29). It has little interest in **keep**(ing) … **the word of God** (v. 28) and his mission (vv. 33-36). Jesus is presenting a **with me …** (or) **against me** (v. 23) scenario. Those who think they disassociate from evil do not. Only those who **hear the wisdom … repent** (vv. 31, 32) are spared **at the judgment** (v. 32).

A Pharisee serves as example of a **body full of darkness** (Luke 11.34). He **was astonished to see that he** (Jesus) **did not first wash before dinner** (v. 38). The fool values outward appearance and overlooks inner realities like **greed … wickedness … neglect**(ing) **justice and the love of God … load**(ing) **people with burdens hard to bear … consent**(ing) **to the deeds of your fathers** who killed the prophets (vv. 39, 42, 46,48). Jesus insults the Pharisees (11.45; 12.1, 2) as they **provoke him** (11.53).

The Pharisee was astonished to see that he did not first wash before dinner (Luke 11.38). Such was his **darkness** (v. 35). Jesus extends his **eye** metaphor (vv. 33-36) to things **inside you** (v. 39) namely, **greed and wickedness** (v. 39). **Teacher … you insult us** (v. 45). Those who **tithe** (v. 42), **build the tombs of the prophets** (v. 47), etc., do not address the true nature of sin and therefore cannot help the common people (v. 52). So

they attack the messenger and **press him hard and ...
provoke ... lying in wait** (vv. 53, 54).

Additional *fool* examples: (1) the man troubled over losing
his portion of an **inheritance** and (2) the man in the parable
resting **in the abundance of his possessions** (Luke 12.13, 15).
Neither is concerned about being **rich toward God** (v. 21).
Jesus teaches anxiety management (vv. 22-31). **Life is more
than food ... more than clothing ... seek his kingdom and
these things will be added to you** (vv. 23, 31). The wise
person has a **heart** (v. 34) for, and **a treasure in the heavens** (v.
33).

hypocrisy ... fear ... blasphem(ing) **against the Holy Spirit
... eat drink and be merry** (Luke 12.1, 4, 10, 19)–not
disparate topics. *Judgment* connects all the material in
chapters 12 & 13. **Nothing is covered up that will not be
revealed** (v. 2) = hypocrisy's phony veil will come down. **Yes,
I tell you, fear him!** (v. 4) = only one fear is justified. **the one
who denies me** (v. 9) **blaspheme** (v. 10) is in the rejection
and denial. **be on your guard against all covetousness** (v. 15)
and instead be **rich toward God** (v. 21).

do not be anxious ... nor be worried (Luke 12.22, 29).
Context: inadequate food and clothing (vv. 22-27). Really?
Cold and hunger are not problems? They are! So what is the
point? **life is more** (v. 23), plus God provides. **God feeds ...
God so clothes** (vv. 24, 28) countless days, until our dying
day. My job: not be **of little faith!** (v. 28); not to be like **all the
nations of the world** (v. 30). Just the opposite: **Sell your
possessions, and give to the needy ...** (from) **your heart** (v.
33, 34).

Stay dressed for action and keep your lamps burning and be like men (Luke 12.35). **Peter said, "Lord are you telling this parable for us or for all?"** (v. 41). Peter did not yet *get it*. What was he thinking? Surely Peter was not *that* self-congratulatory! Jesus brings him back to reality. **Who then is the faithful and wise manager?** (v. 42). Have we not all been **entrusted much** (v. 48)? Serving the Master is life's highest privilege and purpose. A lesser view is not Christian.

be like men who are waiting for their master ... when he comes and knocks (Luke 12.36), i.e. *prepared ... expectant!* Christian living has no room for diversionary pursuits and thoughtless slumber–taking it easy. Rather, it is an intentional, sustainable, balanced, joyful marathon. **Stay dressed for action ... he will dress himself** (vv. 35, 37). Like Jesus, we teach, serve, love and live righteously. **Lord, are you telling this parable for us or for all?** (v. 41). Jesus: **Everyone** (v. 48).

There is a cost: (1) The will of God for Jesus entails crucifixion (Luke 12.50). (2) My pain is far less: **division** (v. 51). As I follow Jesus I will not be walking in the ways of people formerly close, such as family. I can expect them to drop me–or turn on me (vv. 52, 53). I do not repress the pain of these losses, as Jesus did not deny his own suffering. Greater truths occupy the mind: I have an escape from judgment (vv. 47, 48) and **a treasure in heaven** (v. 33).

Jesus can be hard (Luke 12.10, 20, 47)! **I came to cast fire on earth** (v. 49). **I have come to give peace on earth? No ... rather division** (v. 51). Jesus' will and his confrontational teachings are paramount, not civil affairs and personal offenses. **in one house there will be five divided** (v. 52) and at the same time Jesus' followers acquiesce and **settle ... on the way** (v. 58). In both cases, following Jesus is replete with difficulty. He does not soften the teachings but reinforces the need to **repent** (13.3).

When asked to comment on current affairs, Jesus steers conversation back to the eternal. **unless you repent, you will all likewise perish** (Luke 13.3, 5). The more significant news story did not reach the masses: the fig tree without fruit will be cut down (vv. 6-9), a reference to Jerusalem and the populist positions of Herod and the Pharisees (vv. 31-34). By contrast, **the kingdom of God** is like a tree that blesses all around (vv. 18, 19). That kingdom penetrates and expands (vv. 20, 21)!

Before the throne of God there are no **worse sinners ... worse offenders** (Luke 13.2, 4). Nor are there *the privileged.* **unless you repent, you will all likewise perish** (vv. 3, 5). From the penitent, God is **seeking fruit** (v. 7) and Scripture will go on to define just what that means (God's work through the redeemed – John 15.4; Galatians 5.16). The teaching on repentance and fruit represents **the narrow door** (v. 24). Nothing about Jesus' teaching appeals to populism!

Pardon the cliché but actions do speak louder than words. Jesus is teaching on heaven and hell, the status of Israel, and living in the light of his kingdom (Luke 12 & 13). **all the people rejoiced at all the glorious things that were done by him** (13.17). The **hypocrites** (v. 15) took issue with the alleged Sabbath violation. A woman had been healed and **she**

glorified God (v. 13). Few may care about what I profess. On Jesus behalf I bless, heal, help and serve.

Two healings compliment this section of parables and teaching (Luke 13.10-17; 14.1-4). I think Jesus knew the **bent over ... woman** (13.11) in the synagogue would **glorif**(y) **God** (13.13) if healed. **all his adversaries were put to shame** (13.17) for challenging this Sabbath healing. The second challenge was more covert–**they were watching him carefully ... they remained silent ... they could not reply** (14.1, 4, 6). While healing, Jesus teaches (13.15, 16; 14.5).

The **mustard seed** and **leaven** parables (Luke 13.18-21): In a section with stunning instruction (13.3-9; 15-35) and healings (13.13; 14.4), Jesus commends slow, unimpressive growth. Sometimes we see quick interventions. Other times we persevere until **all** (is) **leavened** (13.20)–until **the birds of the air ma**(ke) **nests** (13.19). I can expect confrontation and opposition (13.14, 31; 14.1) while doing my equivalency of going **through towns and villages, teaching** (13.22; cf. 14.23).

Jesus **went to dine at the house of a ruler of the Pharisees** (Luke 14.1) just after blasting the religious establishment (13.31-34). Mission trumps any inclination toward separation and seclusion. Jesus takes control of the conversation. Caught off guard, **they remained silent ... could not reply** (14.4, 6). Jesus confronts **Sabbath** hypocrisy (14.3), social prestige (14.7), and quid pro quo giving (14.12). Such folks **shall not taste my banquet** (14.24). **he who humbles himself shall be exalted** (14.11).

Every human is worthy of recognition, not prestige. What is my interest in **places of honor** (Luke 14.7; cf. 14.8-11) now that I have a worthy Lord to exalt? **sit in the lowest place** (v. 10). What's wrong with that? If I need a little admonition, **everyone who exalts himself will be humbled** (14.11)! For encouragement, some **are last who will be first, and some first who will be last** (13.30). **you will be repaid at the resurrection of the just** ... (and) **shall taste my banquet** (14.14, 24).

He said also to the man who had invited him ... **invite the poor** (Luke 14.12). One disciple *got it*. **Blessed is everyone who will eat bread in the kingdom of God!** (v. 15). The social ranking of the guests by the host (v. 8) left a greater impression on Jesus than the good meal. There are no such distinctions in the kingdom of God and Jesus gives a parable to make that point (vv. 16-24). That message drew **great crowds** (v. 25), which Jesus will now thin out (vv. 26-34)!

they all ... make excuses (Luke 14.18). The world provides a never-ending selection of excuses and distractions, which the sinner is eager to embrace. Convenience, urgency and the low priority over virtue, labor and obedience (which is why human nature needs to be born again – 1 Peter 1.3)! Excuses prompt God to receive glory from new sources (vv. 21, 23), which underscores his grace to those in **the highways and hedges** (v. 23) and his judgment on those requesting, **Please have me excused** (v. 18).

If anyone comes to me and does not hate ... **even his own life, he cannot be my disciple** (Luke 14.26). Jesus and Luke return to the hard theme of *cost* (cf. 9.23-27; 12.49-53). A disciple, like a builder with a construction project, like a king who declares war, cannot be successful if the venture is underestimated (vv. 28-31). He **who does not renounce all that he has cannot be my disciple** (v. 33). We not only fail, we do not even really begin! Jesus has but one kind of disciple!

After **he who is humbles himself will be exalted** (Luke 14.11) and **Blessed is everyone who will eat bread in the kingdom of God** (v. 15), it is no wonder **great crowds accompanied him** (v. 25). The subsequent teaching thins the ranks: **he cannot be my disciple** (v. 26) if possessions (v. 33) or family matters take priority, or if commitment is less than lifetime (vv. 28–32). Without a **cross** (v. 28), the **salt has lost its taste ... It is thrown away** (vv. 34, 35)–mock(ed - v. 29) by the world and **of no use** (v. 35) to Jesus.

After the **cannot be my disciple** (Luke 14.26, 33) teaching comes the **go after the one that is lost** (15.4; cf. vv. 9, 32) teaching. Jesus demonstrates the normalcy of evangelism. **leave the ninety-nine ... seek diligently ...** (15.4, 8); i.e. make the effort. He gives incentives to offset any fear of rejection or opposition: **when one comes home ... Rejoice with me** (15.6). Join **the joy in heaven** ... (the) **joy before the angels** (15.7, 10). **celebrate** (15.29)!

This man receives sinners (Luke 15.2), grumbled the Pharisees and scribes. Jesus takes their observation as *a compliment!* Jesus' teaching turns the Pharisee world up-side-down. He not only receives sinners, he goes looking for them, like a shepherd who goes **after lost the one that is lost until he finds it** (v. 4), or like a woman searching for a

41

misplaced **coin** (v. 8). He / she **calls together ... friends and neighbors, saying "Rejoice with me ..."** (vv. 6, 9). Heaven **rejoice**(s) (vv. 7, 10)!

Note how Jesus describes **the sinners ... Pharisees and scribes** (who) **grumbled** (Luke 15.1,2): **lost** (v. 4, 6, 9, 24), **dead** (vv. 24, 32). **he squandered his property in reckless living ... no longer worthy to be called your son ... a long way off ... devoured your property with prostitutes** (vv. 13, 19, 20, 30). Disgust toward the sinner may have it's reasons but it is not an excuse. The eye of Jesus and the heart of Jesus, not my indignation, is the main issue. The only issue!

Note the united work of the Son–a **man ... having a hundred sheep** (Luke 15.4), the Holy Spirit/Church–a **woman** (v. 8) and the **Father** (v. 11) who all rescue, restore and receive lost sinners (vv. 3-32). The third part of the Luke 15 parable trilogy describes a son being received back by **his father** (vv. 11-32). The feast is the purpose and joy of God (see vv. 6, 7, 9, 10, 22-24, 32), not an aggravating chore. Do not be like the son who does not care to celebrate the return of the prodigal (vv. 28, 29).

After the sections on commitment, sacrifice and evangelism (Luke 13-15), Bible readers are unprepared for the parable of the dishonest manager (16.1-13). **The master commended the dishonest manager for his shrewdness** (16.8). **this man was wasting his** (master's) **possessions** (v. 1), yet was commended. Two points: (1) **make friends** (v. 9). This is an attribute of **One who is faithful** (v. 10). (2) Then God **will entrust you with true riches** (v. 11). **No servant can serve two masters ...** (so) **serve God** (v. 13).

The master commended the dishonest manager (Luke 16.8). Jesus has a compliment for the unscrupulous main character in his parable who was thinking ahead! I need to wisely plan ahead in this life, and for the next (v. 9). A poor use of **unrighteous wealth** (vv. 9, 11) for a believer is a reliable indicator of serving **two masters** (v. 13), which Jesus goes on to say *cannot* be done. **You cannot serve God and money** (v. 13). The guilty are offended (v. 14).

There was a rich man who (Luke 16.1, 19) opens two of Jesus' stories. Jesus also had the antithesis on his mind–**John ... Lazarus** (vv. 16, 20), who juxtapose **The Pharisees, who were lovers of money ... and ... ridiculed him** (Lazarus - v. 14). Jesus cites **The Law and the Prophets ...** (and) **John** (v. 16), martyred for condemning Herod's brother Philip **who had marrie**(d) **a woman divorced from her husband** (v. 18; cf. Mark 6.17-19). Like these Pharisees, people forever try to mold **the good news of the kingdom** (v. 16) to their liking, but to no avail (v. 17).

He who humbles himself will be exalted (Luke 14.11)–case in point, **Lazarus** (16.20): **covered in sores ... desired to be fed ...** (16.20, 21), eating crumbs, cared for by dogs. The exalted rich man arrived at **the place of torment** (v. 28; cf. v. 23). **lovers of money** (v. 14) invariably major on things like feasts and fashion (v. 19), not **Moses and the Prophets** (v. 31). Eternal hope is more apt to be out of focus for the rich than for the poor. The rich man thinks a miracle will turn hearts (v. 30). Think again!

There is a blindness that comes with comfort and security. The wealthy tend not to see the needs and they miss the nature and purpose of life. The **rich man** (Luke 16.19) awakens to reality at death. He nobly asks Abraham to send Lazarus–**someone ... from the dead** (v. 30), to warn his **five brothers** (v. 28) of their folly. To paraphrase **Abraham**, *they already have enough warning in Scripture ... and they would not repent anyway!* (vv. 29-31).

Pay attention to yourselves! (Luke 17.3). After railing **the Pharisees** (and) ... **lovers of money** (Luke 16.14; cf. 16.1, 19), Jesus challenges **his disciples** (17.1). When a **brother sins** (v. 3) I am responsible to **rebuke him ... forgive him** (v. 3). The *forgive* command prompted, **Lord, "Increase our faith!"** (17.5). "You can do it ... (1) **If you have faith** (17.6) and (2) obey–do **what was commanded** (v. 9)." Obedience and forgiveness will be on display in **Jerusalem** (17.11).

Luke 17.1-4 links the problems of (1) setting a bad example and (2) failing to **forgive.** In both cases *I* am the problem. I can be a negative influence; I can bear a grudge. The apostles understood the challenge and appropriately responded, **Increase our faith** (v. 5). God's expectation is not complicated. Combat sinful tendencies as would an **unworthy servant ... do**(ing a) ... **duty** (v. 10). I resign my strong will and make room for the will of God.

The cleansed leper is a positive example. With a full and busy life ahead, **he ... turned back, praising God with a loud voice ... giving him thanks** (Luke 17.15, 16). The clueless Pharisees want to know the *when* of the kingdom! Jesus says this is it–**the kingdom of God is in the midst of you** (v. 21), i.e. *now!* To the disciples Jesus gives a *future* reference–**The** days are coming when you will desire to see one of the days of the Son of Man (v. 22).

More on faith (and **mercy** – v. 13): **your faith has made you well** (Luke 17.19), spoken to the thankful leper, presumably applied by all **ten** (v. 11). Faith in Christ generates miraculous powers, but that was not at issue here. **praising God with a loud voice ... giving him thanks** (vv. 15, 16) was! **The Samaritan** (v. 16) is affirmed for trumpeting the cause (**God**), not the effect (**made well**)! **they were** (all) **cleansed** (v. 14)–a matter of considerable social interest. Jesus lets **the priests** (v. 14) deal with it!

when (would) **the kingdom of God come** (Luke 17.20)? **not ... with signs to be observed** (v. 20). Instead, think praise, healing, serving, forgiving ... (vv. 18, 17, 10, 3; cf. 33). **the kingdom of God is in the midst of you** (v. 21). Now! The end will come suddenly as it did in **the days of Lot** (v. 28) and **Noah** (v. 27). Of greater importance, **the Son of Man ... must suffer many things** (v. 25). **Jerusalem** (v. 11; cf. 13.31-35)! As for us, **whoever loses his life will keep it** (v. 33)–a point missed **by the Pharisees** (v. 20).

when the Son of Man comes (Luke 18.8) indicates Jesus is still thinking about the coming judgment and his return (17.22-37). Nonetheless, he branches out to teach **they ought always to pray and not lose heart** (18.1). Do it! The incentive: **to his elect ... he will give justice to them, speedily** (18.7, 8). Jesus then returns to the coming judgment, condemning pride again (see 17.32)–those **who trusted in themselves** (18.9). **everyone who exalts himself will**

be humbled (18.14). receive the kingdom of God like a child (18.17).

Jesus continues to present kingdom living with positive and negative examples. The widow who kept praying, **give me justice against my adversary** (Luke 18.3) and the **tax gatherer** who prayed, **God, be merciful to me a sinner!** (v. 13), both honor God. As prevailing justice and humility are commended (v. 17), self-congratulations is condemned (18.9-11, 18-21; 20.45-47). The rich ruler *was not* a scoundrel; he *was* too full of himself.

Asking **Why do you call me good?** (Luke 18.19), draws the rich ruler into a losing proposition. No match for Jesus, he **become**(s) **sad** (v. 24) and others who heard the exchange wonder **Then who can be saved?** (v. 26). Jesus corrects their hopeless line of thinking. **What is impossible with men is possible with God** (v. 27). Peter, still thinking he fares well on the scale of good works (v. 28), will be corrected later (22.31), but here is commended. Those who sacrifice **receive many times more in this time and in the age to come** (v. 30).

See, we are going up to Jerusalem (Luke 18.31). Calvary is not many miles away, not many days away. Jesus has not shifted his messianic ministry away from healing, saving and teaching. He responds to the cry of the blind man, **Son of David, have mercy on me!** (18.39). Jesus brings salvation to the tax collector who **climbed up into a sycamore tree to see him** (19.4). He teaches at Zacchaeus' home about the extraordinary importance of commitment and kingdom investment (19.11-28).

The blind man of Jericho **cried out all the more** (Luke 18.39), as if he had heard the teaching *to pray and not lose heart … (to) cry out day and night* (18.1, 7). Sure enough, he **Recover**(ed his) **sight** (through) **faith** (18.42). **all the people … gave praise to God** (v. 43). Those with Zacchaeus, who also received Jesus' special attention, **all grumbled** (19.6). Fickle crowds. Zacchaeus **received him joyfully** (19.6) and is an example. **salvation has come to this house … the Son of Man came to seek and save the lost** (19. 9, 10).

he was near Jerusalem, and … they supposed that the kingdom of God was to appear immediately (Luke 19.11). Jesus and his Father have another plan. The Parable of the Ten Minas reads like an allegory. Jesus will be going **into a far country to receive for himself a kingdom** (v. 12). He leaves behind **his servants … (to) Engage in business** (v. 13)– his business. There is pressure not to do so: **We do not want this man to reign over us** (v. 14). In the end, a **Well done** (v. 17) *or* an **I will condemn you** (v. 22).

As at Jericho, the people in the **Bethpage and Bethany … Mount of Olives** region (Luke 19.28, 37; cf. v. 11) were expectant (vv. 36, 37). Jesus **rode along** (v. 36), fulfilling prophecy (Zechariah 9.9) and receiving opposition (vv. 39, 47). **he wept** (v. 41) and prophesied against **the city** (v. 41): **the days will come upon you, when your enemies will … not leave one stone upon another** (vv. 43, 44). Jesus the prophet causes a ruckus at **the temple** (v. 45) and then teaches (19.46-21.38).

people were hanging on his words (Luke 19.48) while others were **seeking to destroy him** (19.47). A day or so after the rampage in the temple, Jesus returns **preaching the gospel** (20.1). Clearly this was no three-point sermon with an invitation. Rather, he preaches about himself and his kingdom with interaction and stories, such as the parable of the wicked tenants (20.9-18). Jesus' opponents are lurking (20.1, 8, 19, 23, 28, 41; 22.1).

While Jesus teaches **the people** (Luke 20.1, 9), **the chief priests and the scribes** (v. 1; also v. 19) and **some Sadducees** (v. 27) are all nearby. The questions to Jesus feigned innocence (vv. 2, 22, 28). In reality, they **pretended to be sincere** (v. 20)–a trap! (1) Jesus exposes their populism and turns it against them (vv. 3-8). (2) The question about taxes addresses a matter of very little eternal concern (vv. 22-26). (3) The question about eternity–the state of marriage **In the resurrection** (v. 33), receives a thoughtful response.

Jesus' enemies use questions in their effort to entrap him: (1) **Is it lawful to pay tribute to Caesar...?** (Luke 20.22). Not paying is treasonous. Supporting evil violates conscience. Jesus responds, **Render to Caesar** (v. 25). Withholding money from the government is not our issue. (2) **Whose wife will the woman be?** (v. 33). The Sadducees used logic in the attempt to disprove eternal life. Jesus responds that a widow, 7 times over, need not be concerned in heaven about marriage (vv. 34-38).

(3) Another Pharisee question from logic with a matching response from Jesus: **David thus calls him Lord, so how is he his son?** (Luke 20.44) *Son of David* was a well-established messianic reference (18.38, 39) as was Psalm 110 (20.44).

Jesus is cryptically suggesting his divinity and the divinity of Messiah. Let the hearer / reader connect the dots!

"Teacher, you have spoken well." For they no longer dared to ask him a question (Luke 20. 39, 40). Jesus' most able opponents are outmatched. That is when he asks them two questions beyond the scope of their understanding (20.41, 44). Then comes scathing indictments—**devour widows houses and ... pretense** (20.47). Then a "kingdom" observation about the generous **poor widow** (21.3). *She* is the one worthy of notice, not the magnificent and much acclaimed (and short lived - 21.6) **temple ... adorned with noble stones** (21.5)!

I want to see the world through Jesus' eyes. Social prestige and **long prayers** (Luke 20.45-47) have no value. Giving **out of ... poverty** (21.1-4) does! Impressive architecture (v. 5) gives the false impression of permanence and grandeur. **there will not be left ... one stone upon another that will not be thrown down** (v. 6). When the world is falling apart and there is much confusion (vv. 8-26) I must not be **led astray** (v. 8), or **terrified** (v. 9), or discouraged (vv. 34-36). **By your endurance you will gain your lives** (v. 19).

With precious few days remaining, Jesus **was teaching in the temple ...** (from) **early in the morning** (Luke 21.37, 38), beginning with **the end** (v. 9). He was asked about the **sign when these things are about to take place** (v. 7). Jesus gives them four: (1) false messiahs (v. 8), (2) world war (v. 10), (3) natural disasters (v. 11), and (4) persecution (vv. 12-14). Then (5), #s 2&4 converge (vv. 20-24); (6) **they will see the Son of**

Man (v. 27). Endurance (v. 36) is based on hope–**redemption is drawing near** (v. 28).

Luke informs Gentile readers **the Feast of Unleavened Bread … is called the Passover** (Luke 22.1). Despite heightened holiday activity, **the chief priests and the scribes were seeking how to put him to death** (v. 2) as Jesus is the one who **prepare**(s) **the Passover** (v. 8)! **Satan had entered Judas** (v. 3). Jesus had arranged for a **guest room** (v. 11). **in remembrance of me** (v. 19) will come to mean a ceremonial replacement to Passover: **until the kingdom of God comes** (v. 18). **my body … given for you** (v. 19).

In the betrayal of Jesus evil used: (1) long established opposition–people **seeking how to put him to death** (Luke 22.2); (2) **Satan** (v. 3); (3) **money** (v. 5); (4) a willing accomplice–**Judas** (v. 3); (5) secrecy–**an opportunity to betray him … in the absence of a crowd** (v. 6). Expect bad things with any combination of the above. 1 & 2 & 3 are ever-present and unavoidable so always beware. Truth, transparency and benevolence: the best defense … and offense!

With others discussing **who was going to (betray him) … which of them was regarded as the greatest** (Luke 22. 23, 24), Jesus' thoughts are on **the greatest** (:) … **the one who serves** (vv. 24, 27). **let the one who has no sword sell his cloak and buy one** (v. 36) = long-term service requires vigilance and self-defense. Also in the long view, **those who have stayed with me** (v. 28) are rewarded **and sit on thrones judging** (v. 30) while **Satan** (is) **demand**(ing) **… that he might sift** (v. 31)–dissuade from service.

How about that **man carrying a water jar** (Luke 22.10)? The Passover observance begins with mystery. Life has mystery. Who was this man? A servant? One of the **people** (who) **came to him in the temple to hear him** (21.38)? He had access to **a large upper room furnished** (21.12). Was Jesus responding to a previous standing offer of help? Like **the poor widow** (21.2) and **the other women** (24.10), he is a nameless individual just doing his part. I am fine with anonymity.

For who is greater ... ? (Luke 22.27). **Is it not the one who reclines at table** (v. 27)–as the disciples were doing (v. 14)? (1) Like Martha (cf. 10.40), they seemed to have little appreciation for simply enjoying relationship and communication. For Jesus, *that* is the **greatest** (v. 24), not rank! **I earnestly desire to share this Passover with you** (v. 15). (2) There was little appreciation for another kingdom value– service. So Jesus teaches and models, **I am among you as the one who serves** (v. 27).

But this is ... the power of darkness (Luke 22.53), figuratively and literally (cf. 23.44). From darkness come confusion, evil, senselessness and tragedy: (1) The bonds of friendship disappear. Jesus is betrayed by **Judas** (22.47, 48) and denied by **Peter** (22.33, see vv. 54-62; 23.49). (2) Sound teaching is not received. The significance of the Passover is displaced by a quest for greatness (22.14-30). (3) The events are crushing and almost more than Jesus can bear (22.42).

(4) Lies and accusation. After all, Satan is involved! Jesus was not **misleading** (Luke 23.2, 14), opposing taxation (v. 2), or stirring up the people (v. 5). (He *was* **a king** (v. 2)!) **The chief**

priests and the scribes stood by, vehemently accusing him (v. 10). The soldiers and one of the criminals join in (vv. 36, 39). Herod and Pilate feign their ambivalence toward Jesus (vv. 13-15). Jesus' response was hardly a reaction: **weep for yourselves** (v. 28).

Jesus' passion experience is extraordinary, but not atypical. (1) **remove this cup** (Luke 22.42) = "Spare me of pain." (2) **not my will, but yours** (v. 42) = submission to sovereignty. (3) **an angel from heaven strengthening him** (v. 43) = grace received. (4) **being in agony** (v. 44) = the turmoil continues. (5) **the disciples ... sleeping** (v. 45) = no human support. If Jesus was subject to **the power of darkness** (v. 53), no one is immune.

Credit **the power of darkness** (Luke 22.53) for the bizarre events surrounding Jesus' condemnation. He is arrested by **a crowd** (v. 47). **they led him ... into the high priest's house** (v. 54), in the middle of a holiday night! These major events do not obscure Peter's embarrassing denials (vv. 54–62). Jesus' accusers try to terrorize him and **beat** a confession out of him (vv. 63-71). Boldly, they summon the attention of the civil sovereign **Pilate** (23.1), charging Jesus with nothing but words (23.2-5).

Herod and Pilate (Luke 23.12) use the uprise of **The chief priests and the scribes** (v. 10) to schmooze (v. 12). The corrupt Pilate would not accept the **misleading** (v. 14) charge as valid. But he could *be had!* Instead of dismissing evil, he dialogs (vv. 13-25). The unanticipated **release ...** (of) **Barabbas** (v. 18) was the segue to **deliver**(ing) **Jesus over to their will ... as they led him away** (vv. 25, 26). The nearly expired Jesus speaks to those **mourning and lamenting for him** (v. 27): **do not weep for me** (v. 28).

The social scene at Calvary: Jesus continues in magnanimity toward others. **Father, forgive them ... today you will be with me in Paradise** (Luke 23.34, 43; cf. v. 28). This while **the rulers scoffed at him** (v. 35) and **one of the criminals ... railed at him** (v. 39) although **the other rebuked him** (v. 40). The railer and **the crowds that had assembled ... returned home beating their breasts** (v. 48). **his acquaintances ... stood at a distance** (v. 49). Then **a man named Joseph** (v. 50) and **The women** (v. 55) step up.

Why do you seek the living among the dead? (Luke 24.5). What a delightful way to introduce the resurrection era! The **angels** (v. 23) knew all about the spiritual revolution that had just taken place. The 5+ **women** appear to believe (vv. 9, 10). Not the disciples (v. 11). They need evidence. Fair enough. God does not call for empty faith. Reason to believe #1 is the resurrection of Jesus! The account of Jesus' resurrection was written to record history, feed faith and convince the skeptic.

Why do you seek the living among the dead? (Luke 24.5). What kind of a question was this? The women were **perplexed ... dazzl**(ed) **... frightened** (vv. 4, 5). And these **men** (v. 4–*angels, John 20.12*) quiz the witnesses about history's most magnificent event!? Probably spoken with jubilance and some tongue-in-cheek humor. Obviously, the women now had a mission: **they told these things to the eleven and to all the rest** (v. 9)–received as **an idle tale** (v. 11), if not for the events at **the tomb** (v. 12).

What things? (Luke 24.19). Another playful, leading question (see v. 5), this time asked by Jesus in reference to **the things that have happened** (v. 18). The **two ... going to the village named Emmaus** (v. 13) were among those who **did not believe** (v. 11) the women. They were well informed (vv. 19-24) so Jesus chastises them for being **slow of heart to believe** (v. 25). With the conversation on **the Christ ... Moses and all the Prophets ... the Scriptures ... he stayed with them** (vv. 26-29)!

It was a busy Sunday for Jesus. He walked miles and talks with 2 men well aware of the crucifixion and resurrection reports (Luke 24.20-24). He teaches them and accepts a dinner invitation (vv. 26-29). (Note the kingdom values: feeding the mind; hospitality!) It led to **their eyes ... (being) opened** (v. 31). The men return to Jerusalem (7 miles), report to the eleven, and then **Jesus himself stood among them** (v. 36). More teaching and more evidences that though crucified, he lives (vv. 38-49)!

they still disbelieved (Luke 24.41). *Dis*belief is a more serious state than *un*belief. This sinful stronghold is cracked with evidences. The first sign of change is **marveling** (vv. 12, 41), followed closely by **joy** (v. 41). When **eyes ... recogniz**(e) **him** (v. 16), i.e. when **he opened their minds to understand the Scriptures** (v. 45), I presume believers were born. Then comes a responsibility–a commission: proclaim **repentance and forgiveness of sins** (v. 47). **You are witnesses** (v. 48).

To the **startled ... frightened ... troubled ... doubt**(ing) (Luke 24. 37, 38) disciples Jesus says, **Peace to you** (v. 36) and asked, **Have you anything to eat?** (v. 41), **and ate before them**

(v. 43), presumably for social reasons. He then teaches. The disciples need to **understand the Scriptures** (v. 45), particularly **everything written about me** (Jesus – v. 44). Then they receive their commission **to all nations** (v. 47), which will begin after they **are clothed with power from on high** (v. 49; cf. Acts 1.8; 2.4).

Acts of the Apostles

Acts of the Apostles, an historical document with surprising spiritual teachings. Prior to the ascension, Jesus **had given commands ... he ordered them** (Acts 1.2, 4). Christianity / the ministry of the Holy Spirit is the human response to divine commands. The resurrection (v. 3) clearly vested Jesus with supreme authority. Command #1: **wait** (for) **not many days** (vv. 4, 5). **not many** turns out to be 40, which was fine because *timing* was never for them **to know** (v. 7).

Luke wrote of a Jesus very much in charge–**he had given commands ... he ordered them** (Acts 1.2, 4). Resurrection appearances were intentional. **He presented himself alive to them** (v. 3). **the apostles whom he had chosen** (v. 2) were interested in the future: "**Lord will you at this time restore the kingdom** (v. 6)?" So was Jesus: **you will be baptized by the Holy Spirit ... you will be my witnesses** (vv. 5, 8). He then abruptly ascended to heaven!

the two men ... in white robes (Acts 1.10), like *the two men ... in dazzling apparel (Luke 24.4)*, speak about the greatness of Jesus. He **will come in the same way as you saw him go** (v. 11). = When I have questions (see v. 7; Luke 24.4), God may respond with information about himself! With that **the apostles** (v. 2) began their **wait for the promise of the Father** (v. 4), **with one accord ... devoting themselves to prayer** (v. 14), not knowing for how long.

The Father reminds the apostles of Jesus' **authority** (Acts 1.7). The apostles shall be cross cultural, international **witnesses** (v. 8)! Jesus then suddenly is **lifted up ... into heaven** (v. 10). The 11 gather **devoting themselves to prayer** (v. 14). Under higher authority they managed to do this **with one accord** (v. 14). Instead of dwindling, the prayer meeting grew from 11 to **about 120** (v. 15). Peter is then stirred to speak (vv. 16-22).

In those days Peter stood up (Acts 1.15). **those days** followed time **wait**(ing) **for the promise ... devoting** (himself) **to prayer** (vv. 4, 14)–good, precious time. Peter had confirmed that it was **the Holy Spirit** (who) **spoke beforehand by the mouth of David** (v. 16), especially in Psalm 109. **Let another take his** (Judas') **office** (v. 20). So, they commenced with the selection of a 12th apostle. **they cast lots** (v. 26). During that blessed time, I think most any method would be successful.

The apostles replace **Judas** (Acts 1.16-26). The group (11? 120?) suppress their personal preferences regarding the comparable candidates and agree to **cast lots** (1.26). **they prayed, "show which one ... you have chosen ... "** (1.24). It was **Matthias** (1.26). They continued to wait. Jesus was crucified during Passover. Perhaps the Holy Spirit would come (see 1.8) on **the day of Pentecost** (2.1). He did– **suddenly ...** (with) **sound ... to the entire house where they were sitting** (2.2).

I will pour out my Spirit on all flesh (Acts 2.17; Joel 2.28). God fulfills this promise. **the day of Pentecost arrived** (v. 1) with **a sound** (v. 2) and the appearance of **divided tongues as of fire** (v. 3). With this the apostles **were all filled with the Holy Spirit and began to speak in other tongues** (v. 4) about the mighty works of God (v. 11). Then the multitude came together ... amazed and astonished ... and perplexed ... others mocking (vv. 6, 12, 13). This was all early in the morning (v. 15)!

Believers expected to be **baptized ... filled with the Holy Spirit.** (Acts 1.5; 2.4)–not **speak in other tongues** (2.4). **at this sound the multitude came together** (2.6). *Perfect!* The holiday guests heard **Galileans** (2.7) (probably not all 120) speak their **own native language** (2.8). **And all were amazed** (while) **others** (were) **mocking** (2.12, 13). Again, *perfect!* Peter begins his explanation by addressing the mockers (2.14-21).

Peter steps up to offer explanation for the locals (Acts 2.14; cf. 1.15). He cites (1) **what was uttered through the prophet Joel** (v. 16) and (2) **the man attested to you by God with mighty works and wonders and signs ... this Jesus** (vv. 22, 23). (3) **David** (also spoke) **concerning him** (v. 25; cf. vv. 25-28; 34, 35) **and spoke about the resurrection of the Christ** (v. 31)! Before the call to **Repent and be baptized** (v. 38), it was important for all to **know for certain that God had made him both Lord and Christ** (v. 36).

For 40 days believers had been praying together and thinking and talking. The **two men ... in white robes** (Acts 1.10, 11) said Jesus would return. Peter had time to ponder **the last days ... through the prophet Joel** (2.17, 16) which led him to Joel 2.22: **Everyone who calls upon the name of the Lord shall be saved** (2.21). That would be *Jesus!* His life, teachings and resurrection were well known (2.22-24) and also foretold by David (2.25-35). Jesus is **Lord and Christ** (2.36).

they were cut to the heart (Acts 2.37) in the greater context of convincing teaching (vv. 17-36) and undeniable events– **This Jesus God raised up, and of that we are witnesses** (v. 32). Then Peter adds **you will receive the gift of the Holy Spirit** (v. 38; cf. 2.4, 17), a **promise ... for you and your children and for all who are far off, everyone whom the Lord our God calls to himself** (vv. 38, 39). Then **many other words** (v 40). Quite inviting! **three thousand ... received his word** (v. 41).

A great response (Acts 2.41) followed great preaching and great preaching centers on Christ. He was **of Nazareth** (v. 22), a Galilean (!), **with mighty works and wonders and signs ... delivered up ... crucified and killed** (vv. 22, 23). **God raised him up** (v. 24). Then Peter appeals to David **who spoke about the resurrection** (v. 31) and his **exalt**(ation to) **the right hand of God** (v. 33). Then **many other words** (v. 40). More Christology in 3.13, 14, 20-26; 4.1, 2, 10-12.

Brothers, what shall we do? And Peter said to them, "Repent and be baptized ... " (Acts 2.37, 38). The three thousand had outstanding reasons to willingly redirect their lives and commit to Jesus. Stubborn human nature will not overcome the old life with an emotional whim, miraculous sign, or by going along with a believing crowd. God used the truth of Scripture *and* events and they were **cut to the heart** (2.37). They continued the 1.14 pattern of *life together* with prayer and learning (2.42, 44).

about three thousand souls ... were cut to the heart (Acts 2.41, 37) as Peter declared **know for certain that God made him both Lord and Christ, this Jesus whom you crucified** (v. 36). There is power in the truth of Jesus' death and resurrection and the empirical evidence that **the Holy Spirit** (had) **come upon** (1.8) them. This theme will repeat again in chapters 3 & 4. Such is the pattern for the church: prayer, the study of Scriptures, the receiving grace and proclamation of truth.

the promise of the Holy Spirit, he (the Father) **has poured out** (Acts 2.33; cf. v. 17), manifested first in **other tongues** (v. 4), and then **awe** (v. 43) and **wonders and signs ... being done through the apostles** (v. 43). From this spectacular beginning came **all things in common ... selling their possessions and belongings and distributing ... as any had need ... with glad and generous hearts** (vv. 45, 46)! From this the Jerusalem church would drift away. God will reintroduce the ministry of the Holy Spirit to the world in Antioch and through Paul.

This was a time of great grace. People were witnessing (Acts 2.45). **And the Lord added to their number, day by day those who were being saved** (2.47). More signs from heaven: a healing (3.1-10), and another opportunity for Peter to proclaim truth from his mind—which by now has had many weeks intense cultivation. If anything, his preaching is getting better (3.12-26)! Same script: Jesus death and resurrection, supported by Old Testament promises. Peter blames the Jews for rejection.

The pristine Pentecostal church featured miracles (so that others would **see and know ... the faith that is through Jesus** - Acts 3.16) and core teaching (vv. 12-26). (1) Then a miracle: **a man lame from birth was ... made strong** (vv. 2, 7) through Peter who credits **Jesus** (v. 16). **perfect health** (v. 16)! (2) The teaching is warm but confrontational with 10+ statements about Christ (vv. 13-26). **brothers, I know you acted in ignorance** (v. 17). **Repent ... and sins may be blotted out that times of refreshing may come** (v. 19; cf. v. 26).

God ... sent him to you first, to bless you by turning every one of you from your wickedness (Acts 3.26). This great sermon ending resulted in **about five thousand** believers and it **greatly annoyed** (4.2) those who had earlier had condemned Jesus. **They arrested them** (3.3). **They inquired, "By what power or by what name did you do this?"** (3.7). Peter boldly launches into another sermon with the healed man by his side (4.8-14). Outmatched, the best these leaders can do is to call for future silence (4.18). No deal (4.20).

The powerful **Sadducees ...** (were) **greatly annoyed** (Acts 4.1, 2; et al. vv. 5, 6) and quickly found themselves embarrassed before a confident Peter and John **filled with the Holy Spirit** (v. 8) and **five thousand** (v. 4) new believers. Peter shifts the topic from the **crippled man** (v. 9) to **Jesus Christ of Nazareth, whom you crucified, whom God raised from the dead** (v. 10; cf. 5. 30, 31). To that claim they **charged them not to speak or teach** (v. 18; cf. 5.40). And regarding the healing **they had nothing to say** (v. 14).

The believers take their persecution in stride, trusting their **sovereign Lord** (Acts 4.24). The opposition is consistent with

Psalm 2 (vv. 25, 26). The resurrection, the life together of the believers, the signs, the opposition, the boldness–it was all fitting together and feeding off itself as **they had prayed** (and) **the place in which they were gathered together was shaken** (v. 31). **great grace was upon them all** (v. 33).

for all were praising God (Acts 4.21). The church was experiencing an unprecedented season of joy and blessing (see also vv. 32-37). At the same time **the rulers were gathered together against the Lord** (v. 26), *and them!* So much for everything going well! They prayed, **do whatever your hand and your plan has predestined** (v. 28) and continued **to speak the word of God with boldness** (v. 31). Then came **the one heart and soul** (v. 32) resulting in unity and generosity (vv. 32-36).

The events of Act 5 are even more stunning, for *better* and *worse*: (1) **great fear came upon the whole church … many signs and wonders were regularly done … and they all were healed** (vv. 11, 12, 16). **an angel of the Lord opened the prison doors** (v. 19). **they did not cease teaching and preaching** (v. 42). (2) **Satan filled** (Ananias') **heart to lie to the Holy Spirit** (v. 3). **the high priest … arrested the apostles** (vv. 17, 18). **they beat them** (v. 40).

Pretense: an attempt to make one look better than he / she is–**a lie to the Holy Spirit** (Acts 5.3). God received the self-vaunting of **Ananias …** (and) **Sapphira** (vv. 1-10) as a spoiler in his church of purity and power. A *white lie* in this case was actually Satan filling their hearts (v. 3)–a **test** (of) **the Spirit** (v. 9). All things work for the good (cf. Romans 8.28): **great** fear came upon all who heard of it ... the whole church (vv. 6, 10).

God is affirming apostolic ministry and people are responding (Acts 5.12-16). The power hungry, insecure **high priest rose up, and all who were with him (that is, the party of the Sadducees), and filled with jealousy they arrested the apostles** (vv. 17, 18) to no avail (v. 19)! Their release from prison was a miracle of major proportions. The prison is empty and the apostles are teaching **in the temple** (v. 25)! A show down:

Either out of wisdom or cowardice, the guard politely *escorts* the apostles to the high priest, who is sensitive and tired of receiving blame for Jesus' death (Acts 5.28). Peter delivers one great sermon–65 words recorded (vv. 29-32)! **When they heard this, they were enraged and wanted to kill them** (v. 33). Another divine intervention, this time through the much respected **Gamaliel** (v. 34). **I tell you, keep away from these men** (v. 38). After a beating and warning (v. 40), they leave **rejoicing** (v. 41) and undeterred (v. 42)!

And the word of God continued to increase ... and a great many of the priests became obedient to the faith (Acts 6.7)– yet another summary of the church's dynamic beginning and growth. See 2.41; 4.4, 21, 33; 5.14. The **obedient to the faith** description will carry over to Rome (Romans 1.5; 16.26)! Note the *evidences* of the Holy Spirit that precede *the blessing*: (1) Bold proclamation. **Jesus ... you killed by hanging him on a tree ... God exalted him ... to give repentance to Israel** (5. 30, 31).

(2) Joy. they left the presence of the council rejoicing that they were worthy to suffer dishonor (Acts 5.41). (3) Charismata–gifts. pick out from among you seven men of good repute ... full of faith and of the Holy Spirit (6.3, 5). The church (congregation) chose (v. 5) the right people for the task at hand. The emphasis is *not* apostolic or positional authority. This is God's (the church's) method of operation. (4) It is all undergirded by prayer and ... the ministry of the word (6.4).

During the Gamaliel *wait and see* period, there were positive and negative developments: (1) And every day, in the temple and from house to house, they did not cease teaching and preaching that the Christ is Jesus (Acts 5.42). Evangelism is out pacing character development. (2) a complaint by the Hellenists arose ... widows were being neglected (Acts 6.1). No malice was intended but the charge evidently was legit. Again, a problem results in a greater good (6.3, 4). I must expect this!

Acts 6.2-6 has all the elements of a successful conflict resolution: (1) No one was disenfranchised and left out of the process (vv. 2, 5). (2) The conflict does not distract from preaching (vv. 2, 4). (3) men of good repute, full of the Spirit (v. 3) were available. (4) There was much prayer (v. 4). (5) All service is honored (vv. 2, 6) as no one was limited to just serving food (v. 8). God was evidently pleased as the number of the disciples multiplied (v. 7).

Stephen was one of the preachers and miracle workers, and a good one, full of grace and power (Acts 6.8). He was not an apostle but a target of persecution nonetheless. This time non-Judean Jews lead the charge (v. 9), **stir**(ring) **up the people and the elders and the scribes ...** (with) **false witnesses** (vv. 11, 12)–reminiscent of Jesus' arrest. As with Jesus, the accused will dazzle, outwit and outshine his pathetic accusers (Chapter 7).

Extraordinary Steven: **good repute, full of the Spirit and of wisdom ... full of faith ... full of grace and power ... doing great wonders and signs** (Acts 6.3, 5, 8). Unlike apostles Peter and John (5.19), he will not be spared. Stephen's last act leaves a lasting impression. He who was chosen **to serve tables** (6.2) will now speak / preach (7.2-53). Mention of **the Righteous One, whom you have now betrayed and murdered** (7.52) triggers a mob scene (7.57, 58).

Stephen commends his heritage with detail: Abraham bravely **went out from the land of the Chaldeans and lived in Haran** (Acts 7.4) to then have **God remove ... him from there** (v. 4). **he had no child** (v. 5) **his offspring would be sojourners** (and) ... **enslave**(d) (v. 6) and in **great affliction** (v. 11). The bright spot: **Abraham became the father of Isaac and circumcised him** (v. 8). God's plan for the future made / makes the ever-present difficulties all worth it.

Promise offsets hard living–a theme that continues for **four hundred years** (Acts 7.6) including **Jacob** (vv. 9-19) ... **Moses** (vv. 10-43). Stephen will take this conviction to his end. His **God of glory** (v. 2) would reward him with a vision of **the glory of God, and Jesus standing at the right hand of God** (v. 55). Stephen took his stand with **the prophets ...** (and) **the Righteous One** (v. 52), accepting / hastening the same fate.

Like Jesus (Luke 23.34) **he cried out … "Lord, do not hold this sin against them"** (v. 60).

Brothers and fathers, hear me (Acts 7.2). Stephen's boldness did not displace his humility and respect. He may have been testing their patience, as the vv. 3-37 narrative is well known history. Then comes the Deuteronomy 18.15 reference: **God will raise up for you a prophet like me from your brothers** (v. 37). More history in vv. 38-50. Stephen's point: **You stiff-necked people … you always resist the Holy Spirit. As your fathers did, so do you** (v. 51).

they were enraged (Acts 7.54). After all, Stephen was on trial, not them! The nerve! People who trust in their heritage tend to not remember the bad characters and embarrassing events. Truth hurts and gives rise to anger. Stephen has a gruesome (v. 57) yet glorious death. **full of the Holy Spirit, (he) gazed into heaven and saw the glory of God, and Jesus** (v. 55). Full of the Holy Spirit **he cried out with a loud voice, "Lord, do not hold this sin against them"** (v. 60). As he lived, he died– full of boldness, full of grace.

Satan goes for the kill. **And there arose on that day a great persecution against the church in Jerusalem** (Acts 8.1). Many move away (vv. 1, 4, 25), perhaps remembering Jesus' commission (cf. 1.8). The leaders stay to ride out the persecution (vv. 1, 2). God does not skip a beat as Philip effectively teaches and with **signs** (vv. 5-8)! Even the much-acclaimed Simon is impressed and **believes** (vv. 9-13). Simon is a clear example of shallow faith. Sadly, it happens.

they were all scattered throughout the regions of Judea and Samaria, except the apostles (Acts 8.2). Was this good or bad? Either way, the early spread of Christianity was through persecuted believers to the diaspora Jews. Jesus commissioned them to **the regions** (see Matthew 28.19). These Galileans knew cross-cultural ministry. But they would have to also know a universal faith, as Paul did, and as the Judaizers did not (see Galatians 2.4 ff.)

The servants / deacons went. **Philip went down to the city of Samaria and proclaimed to them the Christ** (Acts 8.4). Quality people, *full of faith and the Holy Spirit (6.5),* brought with them proclamation, **signs,** healings, and **much joy** (vv. 6-8)–everything an immature man like **Simon** (vv. 9-24) coveted for himself. Already known as **Great** (v. 10), now a **believe**(r) (v. 13), Simon is positioned for leadership, or so he thought. Ananias and Sapphira did not get past **Peter** (v. 20; cf. 5.1-10); neither will he (vv. 21-24)!

Simon saw that the Spirit was given through the laying on of the apostles' hands, (and) **he offered them money, saying, "Give me this power … "** (Acts 8.18, 19). With this Simon is remembered as one of the great losers in the Bible. Seeking notoriety is a sure way to chase off the unction of the Holy Spirit. Self-exaltation is never a God given purpose. Peter sees the gravity of his folly. **for I see that you are in the gall of bitterness and in the bond of iniquity** (v. 23).

Temper excitement over early professions of faith. **Simon himself believed … after being baptized he continued with Philip** (Acts 8.13). Apparently a very good start. Just apparently. Peter: **you have neither part nor lot in this matter,** for your heart is not right (v. 21). His **heart** defies salvation assurance. This "**believer**" still covets **signs and great miracles** (v. 13) … apostolic authority (v. 19). A fatal flaw. Hopefully Simon gets the point (v. 24)!

God raises up extraordinary people for extraordinary times. And vice versa! Philip is the primary character of Acts 8 and a dynamic leader. He went about **preaching the Word** (Acts 8.4; cf. vv. 5, 12, 35, 40). He was directed **by an angel of the Lord … And the Spirit** (vv. 26, 29) and was the agent of **signs** (v. 6). Where he went, there was **much joy … rejoicing** (vv. 8, 39), not to mention the Samaritan Pentecost (vv. 14-17)! Lord, send us more like him, **full of the Spirit and of wisdom** (6.3).

The evangelism continues (Acts 8.25), coupled with the extraordinary: **Now an angel of the Lord said to Philip** (v. 26). Philip is looking for evangelistic opportunities and finds one. God was opening the heart of **an Ethiopian** (vv. 27-39). His teaching is effective and well received. The penitent welcome baptism (v. 37)! Philip continues on directed– **carried ... (by) the Spirit of the Lord** (v. 39).

The spiritual awakening continues in the north, with accompanying persecution. Saul had devised a way to summon and arrest Jews from Syria and bring them back to the temple court in **Jerusalem** (Acts 9.2). This time it is **Jesus** confronting a fierce opponent of his church (vv. 1, 5). Why Jesus himself appearing? The persecution is *of him!* **suddenly a light from heaven flashed** (v. 3). A revelation so intense **he was without sight, and neither ate nor drank** (v. 9). Saul of Tarsus meets his match!

Saul knew he was a **persecut**(or) (Acts 9.4). He just did not know of whom! It was his **Lord**, i.e. **Jesus** (v. 5), who told him through **Ananias** (v. 10) he would **carry my name before the Gentiles and kings and the children of Israel** (v. 15). Once **filled with the Holy Spirit** (v. 17) and healed (v. 18), he **immediately proclaimed Jesus in the synagogues** (v. 20) with early success, **confound**(ing) **the Jews ... proving that Jesus was the Christ** (v. 22).

for behold, he is praying (Acts 9.11). So begins the converted life of Saul. God sends to him Ananias who lays hands on Saul and pronounces him **filled with the Holy Spirit** (v. 17). Saul **regained his sight ... was baptized ... was strengthened ... and immediately he proclaimed Jesus in the synagogue** (vv. 19, 20). He has a 3-year retreat and study time in Arabia (cf. Galatians 1.17) returning to prove **that Jesus was the Christ** (v. 22).

Days of divine manifestations are met with fiery opposition. Now Saul is on the other side. **The Jews plotted to kill him** (9.23; cf. v. 24). He needs help and receives it from **Ananias ... Judas ... his disciples ... Barnabas** (vv. 10, 11, 25, 27). Preaching **boldly in the name of the Lord ... and disput**(ing) **against the Hellenists** (vv. 28, 29) convinced the skeptical and fearful brothers in **Jerusalem** (v. 26). Despite the threats, **the church ... had peace and was being built up** (v. 31).

Strong characters like Saul have two problems: (1) Would-be friends were all **afraid of him** (Acts 9.26). It was all too much, too fast for the one who had been their sworn enemy. (2) For **preaching boldly ... and disput**(ing) **against the Hellenists ... they were seeking to kill him** (vv. 28, 29). **brothers** help him escape (v. 30). The church is greatly blessed with **peace ... the fear of the Lord and in the comfort of the Holy Spirit** (v. 31).

Peter is serving in roughly the same area as Philip. Through him comes a stunning account of healing and then a raising of the dead (Acts 9.34, 41)! And through this **the residents ... turned to the Lord ... and it became known throughout all Joppa, and many believed in the Lord** (v. 42). Words and deeds result in great credibility. To cancel any doubt about the suitability of Christianity in Sharon, Samaria or any Gentile area, we are given the account of Cornelius (chapters 10 and 11).

Jaw-dropping miracles continue in the area west of Samaria: (1) At the prayer of Peter, **Aeneas, bedridden for eight years ... rose** (Acts 9.33, 34)! Not **surprisingly all the residents of Lydda and Sharon ... turned to the Lord** (9.35). (2) By now there were **disciples** (9.38) on the coast in **Joppa** (9.36) who send for Peter to raise a woman who **became ill and died** (9.36). He came and then **presented her alive** (9.41)! (3) Peter's next summons comes from **the Spirit** (10.19) and **three men** (10.19) from **Caesarea** (10.1).

a devout man ... (who) feared God ... gave alms ... prayed continually ... well spoken of (Acts 10.2, 22), Cornelius is not far from the kingdom of God. But he is 35 miles from Peter, whom he summons, as the angel instructed. **The next day** (v. 9) Peter's hunger turns into a trance and he is told to eat **unclean** animals (vv. 13, 14). God is overruling the custom that **a Jew ... (should not) associate with or ... visit anyone of another nation** (v. 28). God hammers that sin with a powerful demonstration:

(1) **accompany them without hesitation** (Acts 10.20). Note all the loving effort done for the sake of individuals (see 9.32, 39)! (2) There seems to be a connection between the people (who) **prayed continually to God** (v. 2) and Peter seeing **the heavens open** (v. 11). (3) The miracle-agent Peter is still *a piece of work* himself with much to learn (vv. 10-16)! **God has shown me that I should not call any person common or unclean** (v. 28).

hungry (Acts 10.10) Peter learns about Cornelius, himself *starving* **to hear what** (he has) **to say** (v. 22). This was the angel's idea and for a purpose much more information! His **prayer** and giving of **alms** (v. 31) prompted a visit from **a holy angel** (v. 22; cf. v. 30) who directs him to **bring one Simon who is called Peter** (v. 5) **to hear what** (he has) **been commanded by the Lord** (v. 33). Cornelius receives a gospel presentation (vv. 34-43) and **the Holy Spirit** (v. 44).

Peter's *nightmare* **happened three times** (Acts 10.16): **"Rise Peter; kill and eat"** ... **(the) common and unclean** (vv. 13, 14; cf. v. 28). The "unclean" Cornelius **wanted to hear what** (he had) **to say** (v. 22). Peter **and some of the brothers from Joppa ... entered Caesarea** (vv. 23, 24) and present **the good news of peace through Jesus Christ (he is Lord of all)** (v. 36; cf. vv. 34-43). **the Holy Spirit fell on all who heard the word** (v. 44).

You yourselves know what happened throughout all of Judea (Acts 10.37). Cornelius, like all converts, first accepts the testimony of Jesus' life, teaching, death and resurrection (vv. 37-41). As the implications of lordship are being explained (vv. 42, 43) **the Holy Spirit fell on all who heard the word** (v. 44). It was **the gift of the Holy Spirit ...** (with) **speaking in**

tongues and extoling God ... just as on us at the beginning (10.45, 46; 11.15). Conversion defined: **Gentiles ... had received the Word of God** (to whom) **he granted repentance that leads to life** (11.1, 18).

Truly, **the Holy Spirit fell** (Acts 10.44) upon the right person, **a devout man who feared God ... and prayed continually** (v. 1). Cornelius was eager **to hear all** (Peter had) **been commanded** (v. 33), which was a review of current events (vv. 36-42). (Jewish theology was predominantly a historical remembrance!) **you yourselves know what happened ... we are witnesses of all he did** (vv. 37, 39). V. 43 is the application: **the prophets bear witness that everyone who believes in him receives forgiveness.**

Peter was flanked by believers **from among the circumcised** (Acts 10.45), to be known as **the circumcision party** (11.2). Some of them in **Jerusalem ... criticized him saying, "You went to uncircumcised men and ate with them"** (11.2, 3)–an incongruent response in light of 10.44-48! Once again, in good Jewish form, Peter simply recounts what happened (11.4-17), attested by **These six brothers** (11.12). His critics then provide the conclusion: **to the Gentiles also God has granted repentance that leads to life** (11.18).

Christianity is now clearly universal. Between Jew and Gentile there is **no distinction** (Acts 11.12). **the Holy Spirit fell on them** (Gentiles - v. 15). Who **could stand in God's way?** (v. 17). Not all *got it!* **the circumcision party criticized him** (Peter - v. 2). **those who were scattered ...** (were) **speaking the word to no one except Jews** (v. 19). Meanwhile **men of Cyprus and Cyrene ... spoke to Hellenists ... and a** great number who believed turned to the Lord (vv. 20, 21) in Antioch. Credit **the grace of God** (v. 23)!

God had responded with power in response to **the persecution** (Acts 11.19). Gentiles were being reached in Antioch in **great number** (v. 21). Barnabas likes what he sees (v. 23). **full of the Holy Spirit and of faith** (v. 24) he goes **to Tarsus to look for Saul** (v. 25). During the next year believers receive great teaching, numerical growth and a new name– **Christians** (v. 26)! Not surprisingly, they are generous (vv. 27-30; cf. 4.34-37).

Barnabas served the church by **preaching the Lord Jesus** (Acts 11.20), **exhort**(ing) **them all to remain faithful to the Lord with steadfast purpose** (v. 23), going **to Tarsus to look for Saul** (v. 25) and bringing him to Antioch to teach (v. 26). Prophets came to Antioch, surprisingly **from Jerusalem** (v. 27), with a word about a coming **great famine** (v. 28) and how they could respond. **Barnabas and Saul ... (bring) relief to the brothers living in Judea** (vv. 30, 29).

great famine (Acts 11.28) and now **the sword** (12.1)! Powerful **Herod the king** (12.1) was intimidated by John the Baptist and now by the Christians, who were wielding a different kind of power. He begins a campaign to eliminate the apostles–**James ... Peter** (12.2) **during the days of Unleavened Bread** (12.3), reminiscent of the Holy Week violence. **earnest prayer ... by the church of God** (12.5) prompts a rescue through **an angel of the Lord** (12.7), despite **the two chains, and sentries before the door** (12.6).

Churches experience persecution, divine intervention and joy. Herod kills an apostle (Acts 12.1). **he proceeded to arrest Peter also** (v. 3). **earnest prayer for him was made** (v. 5). **an angel** releases a dazed Peter from his cell (vv. 7-12), for which the guarding sentries are **put to death** (v. 19). An **amazed** (v. 16) church at the house of Mary receives Peter with joy but he wisely keeps moving. The wicked, dangerous and pompous Herod is **struck down ... by an angel of the Lord** (v. 23).

the Word of God increased and multiplied (Acts 12.24) despite the persecution and famine. **Barnabas and Saul** (12.25) laid low during the events of chapter 12 but that will change as they return to the **worshiping ... and fasting ... church at Antioch** (13.2, 1). Credit **the Holy Spirit** (13.2), the Word of God and a responsive church for the dynamism! Barnabas and Saul continue their travels together as Peter and Philip had before them.

Everyone ends up either on the right or wrong side of history. Affirmed in Acts 12 are **James, brother of John ... Peter ... Mary ... Rhoda ... James ... Blastus ... Barnabas and Saul** (vv. 2, 12, 13, 19, 20, 25)–people who were **praying** (v. 12) and **serv**(ing) (v. 25). **the word of God increased and multiplied** (v. 24). **Herod**, is the loser (vv. 19-23). He was as shallow (vv. 2, 22), vengeful (vv. 19, 20), and pompous (v. 21) as he was wealthy and powerful–a waste at *the top of the heap.*

The acts of the apostles combine human initiative (obedience, courage, service) and divine provision (angels, miracles, guidance). This combination remains the norm. To the exemplary, diverse, gift oriented, responsive **church at**

Antioch (Acts 13.1), **the Holy Spirit said** (v. 2)! **Barnabas and Saul** (were to be) ... **sent out by the Holy Spirit** (vv. 2, 4). God moves those on the move and moves with the movers! The church must not calcify with routines, policy and ritual (v. 2).

The mission to the Gentiles begins with **proclaim**(ing) **the word of God in the synagogues** (Acts 13.4) with no recorded response or results until they travel another 100 miles. **the proconsul, Sergius Paulus** (v. 7) is interested while **Elymas ... opposed them seeking to turn the proconsul away from the faith** (vv. 7, 8). This **son of the devil** (v. 10) is powerfully checked by Saul, who pronounces his blindness. Elymas is humbled, **seeking people to lead him** (v. 11). Sergius Paulus is more impressed with the proclamation–**astonished at the teaching of the Lord** (v. 12)!

Paul and his companions set sail ... to Perga (Acts 13.13) and travel another hundred miles **to Antioch in Pisidia** (v. 14), with no recorded results. **John left them** (v. 13), presumably because of the many difficulties. The rulers of the synagogue requested **any word of encouragement for the people** (v. 15). Luke records the subsequent sermon (vv. 16-41): a historical prologue (vv. 16-26) and the **message of ... salvation** (v. 26)– **God raised him** (Jesus) **from the dead** (v. 30).

Paul was invited to bring **a word of encouragement** (Acts 13.15) to those in the synagogue of Pisidian Antioch. His sermon is much like Stephen's (cf. chapter 7), reviewing highpoints of Jewish history (13.17-23). Unlike Stephen, he includes messianic references (vv. 32-41), the fact of Jesus' resurrection (vv. 30-35), and an evangelistic appeal: **through** this man forgiveness of sins is proclaimed ... everyone who believes is freed (vv. 38, 39). There is a great response (v. 43)!

It gets even better ... and worse! **Gentiles ... rejoicing and glorifying the word of the Lord ... many as were appointed to eternal life believed. And the word of their Lord was spreading throughout the whole region** (Acts 13.48, 49). The many opposers **stirred up persecution** (v. 50). Nonetheless **the disciples were filled with joy and with the Holy Spirit** (v. 52). A church in revival will have *blessings and bombs* aplenty!

This missionary journey tracks three active players: (1) God **appoint**(ing **many**) **to eternal life ... bearing witness to the word of his grace, granting signs and wonders** (Acts 13.48; 14.3); (2) **the disciples were filled with joy and with the Holy Spirit** (13.52), **speaking boldly** (14.3), **while fleeing** (14.6; cf. 13.51); (3) **rulers** (14.5)–women of high standing and the leading men of the city stirred up persecution (13.50) ... even attempting **to stone them** (14.5).

Boldness: **Paul, looking intently** ... saw the **crippled** man ... **had faith to be made well** (Acts 14.8, 9) and pronounced his healing (v. 10). **Barnabas and Paul** (v. 14) divert credit from themselves to the **living God** (v. 15) with bold preaching / teaching. **nations ... walk ... in their own ways. Yet he** (God) **did not leave himself without witness** (vv. 16, 17)–*the gospel of creation* (vv. 15-17). For this and the bold message of 13.38, 39, out-of-towners **persuaded the crowd** (mob), **and they stoned Paul** (v. 19).

There is no break in this pattern: effectual ministry followed by persecution. **a great number … believed … unbelieving Jews stirred up the Gentiles and poisoned their minds.** (Acts 14.1, 2). In response: **they remained a long time, preaching boldly for the Lord who bore witness to the word of his grace** (v. 3). The attempt **to stone** (v. 5) Paul and Barnabas at Iconium is successful at Lystra (v. 19). Great preaching (vv. 9-18), resolve (vv. 23, 24, 28), growth (vv. 21-23), and **many tribulations** (v. 22) mark the first missionary journey.

Encouragement is a companion ministry to proclamation. From **Derbe** (Acts 14.20), 200 miles from home, **they returned to Lystra** (v. 21)–the opposite direction from home– and continue to retrace their steps (vv. 21, 24-26), **strengthening the souls of the disciples, encouraging them** (vv. 21, 22; cf. 13.15, 43): **through many tribulations we must enter the kingdom of God** (v. 22). Paul and Barnabas **committed them to the Lord** (v. 23), then they were **commended to the grace of God** (v. 26).

This was a time a great blessing and peril. Acts 14.24-28 emphasizes the blessing. God was mightily at work, opening doors to the Gentiles with an extended time of fellowship in Antioch. However, the gospel was under severe attack both from the mission field (14.24, 25; cf. Galatians 1.6) and the home bases of Antioch and Jerusalem (15.1, 5). The issue: **you cannot be saved …** (unless you) **keep the law of Moses** (15.1, 5). The tone of The Jerusalem Council debate is commendable. The elders **considered the matter** (15.6).

some men came down from Judea … some believers who belonged to the party of the Pharisees rose up (Acts 15.1, 5).

77

History remembers them as people bringing their luggage to Christianity–in this case, prior religious convictions. **Paul and Barnabas** (v. 2) gave reasons aplenty to accept *the fellowship of the Holy Spirit* church model, having **declared all that God had done** (v. 4). **the apostles and the elders** (v. 6), not that they had made up their minds, proceed with grace and diplomacy (15.6ff).

Acts 15.7-12 reveals Peter's understanding of the good news (cf. 11.17). **we will be saved through the grace of the Lord Jesus** ... (without) **putting God to the test by placing a yoke on the neck of the disciples** (15.11, 10)–religious, cultural. James concurs, **we should not trouble those of the Gentiles who turn to God** (v. 19). **but** (v. 2) with consideration to the Jews **in every city** (v. 21), **keep the law of Moses** (v. 5) in some tangible ways (v. 20). This outcome **seemed good** (v. 21) in Jerusalem and **they rejoiced** (v. 31) in Antioch.

Therefore My judgment is we should not trouble those Gentiles who turn to God (Acts 15.19). Respectful and diplomatic James presents the position that will prevail. The Judaizers have a tight argument and sound logic but the elders believe God does not agree. Gentiles had received **the Holy Spirit** (v. 8), salvation (v. 11), **signs and wonders** (v. 12), as God was fulfilling his promise to **rebuild the tent of David** (v. 16) with **Gentiles** (v. 17), who will in turn show respect to moral and some ceremonial law (vv. 20, 21).

The apostolic letter was **from the brothers ... to the brothers** (Acts 15.23)–i.e. familial and collegial. The Antioch missionaries, **our beloved** (v. 25) **Judas and Silas** (v. 27), accompany the letter. Another sign of good will was the 4

requirements (v. 28), covering social, priestly and moral concerns. With the **no greater burden** (v. 28), compliance should not be a problem. **Judas and Silas ... encouraged and strengthened the brothers** (v. 32). The letter was an **encouragement** (v. 31).

Let us return and visit the brothers ... and see how they are (Acts 15.36). Paul's desire for fellowship motivated his second mission trip. He and Silas would head for their earlier turn-around point (Derbe), while Barnabas and John Mark return **to Cyprus** (15.37-39). Truly the churches were **strengthened** (15.40; 16.5). **Timothy** and Luke join Paul's party (16.3, 10). Having won the theological battle in Jerusalem (15.19), he is happy to have Timothy **circumcised** (16.3; cf. 15.20, 28; 16.4) to gain initial acceptance from the Jews. Hopefully Timothy was also happy about that!

Paul thought it best not to take with them ... John called Mark (Acts 15.38, 37). **Paul chose Silas** (15.40). **Paul wanted Timothy to accompany him** (16.3). Nonetheless, he still appeals to **the brothers** (15.40) for commendation. The emphasis was on **strengthening the churches** (15.41; cf. 16.5) and with that **they increased in numbers daily** (16.5).

having been forbidden by the Holy Spirit (Acts 16.6). These gift-based Antioch believers were dependent on prayer and prophecy for direction. Their attempts to enter **Asia** (and) **Bithynia** (vv. 6, 7) were receiving no intuitive support. Amidst the quandary, **a vision (of) ... a man from Macedonia** (v. 9) urged them to enter Europe–new territory. They considered the vision and concluded that **God had called** (v. 10). Lessons: (1) I need *not* have a long-term plan; (2) when I do, God may change it; (3) I must always be active and engaged.

The heretofore pro-active Holy Spirit now says, "no." Paul and company were **forbidden by the Holy Spirit to speak the word in Asia ... the Spirit of Jesus did not allow them** (Acts 16.6, 7). Noes lead to yesses. **God had called us to preach the gospel to them** (v. 10) in Macedonia but with no recorded results in **Samothrace ... Neapolis** (v. 11) and even Philippi for **some days** (v. 12). Success came **outside the gate** (by) **the riverside ... to the women who had come together** (v. 13), actually one woman who had **opened her heart** (v. 14). In God's kingdom events like this are huge!

outside the gate to the riverside ... there was a place of prayer ... (with) **women who had come together** (Acts 16.13). No compulsion or obligation. Their heart's desire was to pray ... **together** ... and *this* is where God chooses to work–then and now! The able **Lydia** becomes a solid convert and disciple (vv. 14, 15)! God works again as Paul's party is en route to another prayer meeting. **a slave girl who had a spirit of divination** (v. 16) was set free (v. 18). But her owners charged, **they are disturbing our city** (v. 20). More trouble!

It was likely torment that brought the **slave girl with a spirit of divination ... to the place of prayer** (Acts 16.16). She was **annoy**ing (vv. 17, 18), yet received Paul's pity and a demonstration of God's power (v. 18). Her offended owners, not mentioning **their hope of gain was gone** (v. 19), charge Paul and Silas with social and legal violations (vv. 20, 21). There was nothing legal about **The crowd ... attacking** them, and the magistrates ... inflict(ing) **many blows** (v. 22). No mention of **Roman citizen**(ship) (v. 37).

By now Paul and Silas see persecution more as the norm than an occasional crisis. Undeterred from a severe beating and miserable prison conditions (Acts 16.23, 24), they **were praying and singing hymns to God** (v. 25). Suddenly **all the doors were open and everyone's bonds were unfastened** (v. 26). Expecting condemnation for the collapse of his prison, the jailor asks, **What must I do to be saved?** (v. 30). Paul moves the conversation to his spiritual condition, **Believe in the Lord Jesus** (v. 31).

With torn **garments**, many wounds, a dark **inner prison ... feet in stocks**, the suffering **Paul and Silas are singing hymns to God** (Acts 16.22-25)–amazing, as was the **great earthquake** (v. 26), which effectively destroyed the prison! The jailor, principled ... reliable, **tremble**(ed) **with fear** (and) **fell down before Paul and Silas** (v. 29). He and his household were quick converts (vv. 31-33). **he rejoiced ...** (because) **he had believed in God** (v. 34).

Characteristics of Christianity: (1) **So they ... visited Lydia** (Acts 16.39). **and when they had seen the brothers, they encouraged them** (v. 40). *Lots of fellowship!* (2) **Paul ... reasoned with them from the Scriptures** (17.2) in Thessalonica. Berean **Jews were ... examining the Scriptures daily** (17.11). *Teaching centered.* (3) A Thessalonian **mob, set the city in an uproar** (17.5), **then agitating and stirring up the crowds** (17.13; cf. 16.39) in Berea. *Fierce opposition!*

Opponents of Christ are sensitive (Acts 16.20; 17.6, 7, 13) and wicked (17.5). Deliverance from trouble is an oft-repeated theme, as is the ministry of **the word of the Lord** (16.32)–**reason**(ing) ... **from the Scriptures** (17.2), and **examining the Scriptures daily** (17.11). The new converts here are people of high standing (16.15, 33; 17.4, 12) and are given much to believe in! Believers are **baptized** (16.33), **join** ... (17.4), and help (17.15).

Examples of how the sovereign God saves: (1) After the earthquake, the *believing* Philippian jailor got more specific and believed **in the Lord Jesus Christ** (Acts 16.31). (2) In Thessalonica Jews and Greeks **were persuaded** (17.4) **Jesus** (was) **the Christ** (17.3; cf. v. 34). (3) Bereans **received the word with all eagerness** (17.11). But before this, much **explaining and proving** (17.3; cf. v. 17) takes place. 17.22-31 is a case in point.

Now while waiting ... his spirit was provoked (Acts 17.16) and opportunities to reason and converse with a diverse group (vv. 17, 18) were presented in the Athens marketplace and civil courtyard (vv. 17, 22). Good evangelism connects with the world of the listener. Paul addresses **the object of your worship** (v. 23), **the God who made the world and everything** (v. 24), and **some of your own poets** (v. 28). He then relates this to judgment day and **the man** (whom God) **rais**(ed) **from the dead** (v. 31).

Rejection continued from the religious (Acts 17.5, 13; 18.6) **in the synagogue** (18.4) and from the philosophers (17.21, 32) in new venues–**the marketplace ... Areopagus** (17.17, 19). When Paul commits **From now on I will go to the**

Gentiles (18.6), he is led to **Crispus, the ruler of the synagogue, (who) believed in the Lord Jesus, together with his household** (18.8). Delightful! Paul obeys a vision (18.9, 10) and **stayed a year and six months** (18.11) in Corinth.

From now on I will go to the Gentiles (Acts 18.6). In Corinth, Paul appears to give up on the Jews. That is when **Crispus, the ruler of the synagogue believed in the Lord, together with his entire household** (v. 8). God had not given up on the Jews, or on Paul for his mistaken understanding. Paul receives a vision: **I have many in this city who are my people** (v. 10). If in Corinth, why not every city! Then **the Jews made a united attack** (v. 12) and poor **Sosthenes** is unjustly beaten (v. 17). Guilt by association.

no one will attack you or harm you ... the Jews made a united attack (Acts 18.10, 12). The latter **attack** was a trumped up legal complaint. **Gallio paid no attention to any of this** (18.17). 18.18-19.1 is a short section that covers the long trip from Greece to Caesarea to Antioch to Ephesus with many more stops in **Galatia and Phyrgia** (v. 23). Teaching in the synagogue continues to be the primary strategy, both for Paul and Apollos (18.19, 28; 19.8), who also **reasoned daily in the Hall of Tyrannus** (19.10).

he greatly helped those who through grace believed (Acts 18.27). It is easy to see why Apollos was effective. He was, **an eloquent man, competent in the Scriptures ... fervent in spirit ... encouraged** (by the brothers and) **... powerfully refuted the Jews in public** (vv. 24, 25, 27). Nonetheless, he needs the correcting help of **Priscilla and Aquila** (v. 26) and then Paul, who then introduces the Ephesian believers to the reality of **the Holy Spirit** (19.2-7). This apparently had not been taught by Apollos, or on the earlier visit from Paul (18.19, 20).

Surprising occurrences continue: (1) **John** had followers and international respect in distant regions (Acts 19.1-4). (2) **the Holy Spirit came on them, and they began speaking in tongues and prophesying** (v. 6) upon believing in Jesus. Paul then **spoke boldly ... reasoned daily** (vv. 8, 9) for 27 months, complete with miracles and healing (vv. 11, 12). **Jewish exorcists** are embarrassed by **the evil spirits** the apostles cast out (vv. 13-16). What a Bible institute this was! **And fear fell upon them all** (v. 17) as **the word of the Lord ... prevail**(ed) **mightily** (v. 20).

The Ephesian ministry was exemplary. The church (1) **receive**(d) **the Holy Spirit** (Acts 19.2) and (2) was learning from Paul's **reasoning and persuading ... reasoning daily** (vv. 8, 10). (3) **all the residents of Asia heard the** word (v. 10; cf. v. 20). (4) **God was doing extraordinary miracles** (v. 11). (5) **evil spirit**(s) (v. 16) were overcome (vv.13-16). (6) Many repented of their occult interest with a costly book burning (vv. 18-20). (7) The world received this as **no little disturbance** (v. 23) resulting in a riot (vv. 24-40).

The local religion had taken a hit (Acts 19.19, 23-27) and responds with force. **Demetrius** (v. 24) addresses economics–his last remaining apologetic. Orderly proceedings are impossible once a mob forms (vv. 33, 34). After two hours of hoopla, the **town clerk** (v. 35), no small office holder, quiets them down with the threat of Roman intervention (v. 40). The gutless troublemakers simply go home (v. 41). Paul considers the persecution outbreaks in determining his travel plans (20.3). His travels continue.

a plot was made against him (Paul) (Acts 20.3) yet again! Offering much encouragement (v. 2) is the only recorded "offense"! Six new travelling companions are not deterred (vv. 4-6). Paul sailed away from Philippi (v. 5). One evening in Troas, Paul prolonged his speech until midnight ... talked still longer (v. 7, 9) then with a willing audience conversed until daybreak (v. 11), including the Eutychus incident—one who was taken up dead (v. 9) then took ... away alive (v. 12). Remarkable!

We stayed for seven days. On the first day of the week, when we were gathered together to break bread, Paul talked with them (Acts 20.6, 7). The context of the mission in Troas was fellowship–enjoying the presence of one another (cf. vv. 37, 38). One night it got late and sleepy Eutychus (v. 9) had a deadly fall. As he was raised, all were not a little comforted (v. 12). Despite this *open door,* Paul is constrained to be at Jerusalem, if possible, on the day of Pentecost (v. 16), close to the 20th anniversary of Acts 2.

In Troas Paul conversed with them a long while (Acts 20.11). In Ephesus he said to them: Your yourselves know how I lived (v. 18). = Extensive teaching and lifestyle example are the ingredients to effective evangelism, church planting, discipling ... just about everything! People saw in Paul one serving the Lord with all humility and with tears and trials (v. 19). He had an objective (15.36; 16.10; 18.9; 20.20, 21) but little control over the details and timing. Just testify to the gospel of grace ... declare the whole counsel of God (20.24, 27)!

The exemplary Christian: **serving the Lord with all humility and with tears and with trials** ... I did not shrink from declaring to you anything that was profitable ... and teaching ...repentance toward God and of faith in our Lord Jesus Christ ... constrained by the Spirit, not knowing what will happen to me ... I do not account my life of any value nor as precious to myself, if only I may finish my course and the ministry that I received from the Lord Jesus, to testify to the gospel of the grace of God ... proclaiming the kingdom (Acts 20.19-25).

Ministry essentials: (1) **admonish everyone with tears** (Acts 20.31). (2) **covet no one's silver or gold or apparel** (v. 33). (3) **by working hard ... help the weak** (v. 35). (4) **pray with them all** (v. 30; cf. 21.52). (5) seek direction **through the Spirit** (21.4; cf. 21.11). (6) Paul wanted to follow Jesus quite literally, even to **die in Jerusalem** (21.13). (7) Finally, Paul was not headstrong so as to rebuff counsel. He concedes to those **zealous for the law** (21.20) and **purified himself** ... (in) **the temple** (21.26).

Exemplary Christian service continued: **I did not shrink from declaring to you the whole counsel of God** ... care for the church of God, which he obtained with his own blood ... be alert ... admonish every one with tears ... coveted no one's silver or gold or apparel ... by working hard in this way we must help the weak and remember the words of the Lord Jesus, how he himself said, 'It is more blessed to give than to receive … he knelt down and prayed with them all (Acts 20.27-36).

Acts 21.1-17 is a fine example of first century Christian living. Paul and company are traveling. (1) No pre-planning (vv. 1-3). They must make arrangements on the road and at sea. (2) **having sought out the disciples, we stayed there for seven days** (v. 4). There is plenty of hospitality and mutual love. Sometimes the guest list was extensive (vv. 16, 17)! (3) Prophecy and prayer (v. 9): **through the Spirit they were telling Paul not to go on … And kneeling down on the beach, we prayed … 'Thus says the Holy Spirit …** (vv. 4, 11).

Paul was certain in **Jerusalem … imprisonments and afflictions await** (Acts 20.23). **the disciples** (21.4) in Tyre and **Agabus** (21.10) confirm, **urg**(ing) **him not to go** (21.12). Bravely, **some of the disciples from Caesarea went with** (21.16) Paul and Luke. **many thousands** (21.20) had become believers there but were **zealous for the law** (21.20), which spared them from persecution. **all the city was stirred up** (21.30). They **laid hands on him … dragged him out of the temple … seeking to kill him** (21.30, 31).

Having accepted the Antioch model of church polity and taking a step away from Judaizers, Paul and the elders now had to deal with the **many thousands … among the Jews … who have believed** (Acts 21.20) and were expecting *all* to **walk according to our customs** (v. 21). Paul had won the doctrinal war (v. 25). He would now gladly concede a battle, **shav**(ing) **heads** (vv. 24, 26), inconsequential to him but meaningful to the Jerusalem church. But bringing

Trophimus (v. 29) into the temple was evidently a mistake, triggering another **mob** scene and riot (vv. 30-36).

all Jerusalem was in confusion (Acts 21.31) and the **mob ... (was) crying out, "Away with him!"** (21.36). **they stopped beating Paul** (21.32) as soldiers **actually carried** (him) ... **into the barracks** (21.35, 37). A remarkably composed Paul tells his story (22.2-21) **in the Hebrew language** (21.40), i.e. addressing his accusers! His support of **Stephen** (22.20) reignited the mob, which signaled **that he should be examined by flogging to find out why they were shouting** (22.24). The world does not promise justice.

I beg you, permit me to speak ... there was a great hush (Acts 21.29, 30). This was not a conflict to avoid but an opportunity (with risk)! Paul tells his story: his shameful past, conversion, his vision and his calling (22.3-21). It was stories that had earlier persuaded the Jerusalem Council (15.12). When Paul got to the **to the Gentiles** (22.21) part, the tribune gave their verdict: **he should not be allowed to live** (22.22). A problem? Well, he just missed another beating but *did* get yet another speaking opportunity (Chapter 23).

If anything, Paul had more intense opposition in Jerusalem than did Jesus! Pilate and Caiaphas were plenty guilty. **the high priest Ananias** (Acts 23.2; cf. 24.1-7) was more corrupt and vengeful. Paul uses irony to contrast the office with the man occupying that office (v. 5). (Ananias himself will soon be summoned to Rome to answer charges!) Despite the danger, Paul once again is a composed, courageous and clever defendant, playing on the **Pharisee ... Sadducee** differences (vv. 6-8).

Paul out-maneuvers his opponents. Once he learns they will not listen, he scores in the tiff with **Ananias** (Acts 23.1-5) and then turns the **Sadducees and … Pharisees** against one another (vv. 6-10). Not appreciated! **the Jews made a plot and bound themselves by an oath neither to eat nor drink till they had killed Paul** (v. 12). The Roman tribune learns of this and refers Paul and his case to **the governor** (v. 24). They clandestinely transport Paul to **Caesarea** (vv. 23, 33).

There is little doctrine and little Jesus present in Acts 22.17-26.11. Rather the topic is Paul, navigating his defense and survival. *In his favor:* **they did not find me disputing with anyone or stirring up a crowd … I have done no wrong … there is nothing in their charges against me … nothing deserving death … I am speaking true and rational words** (24.12; 25.10, 11, 25; 26.25). *Against him:* the relentless accusations from intolerant Jews, with **the high priest Ananias** leading the charge, traveling 50 miles to Caesarea (24.1), to settle a grudge (23.1-5).

The most eloquent **Tertullus** (Acts 24.1) presents the charge against Paul. First he *kisses up* to Felix (vv. 2-4). Then come the *almost* convincing accusations, hampered only by a lack of facts. **We have found this man a plague …** (he) **stirs up riots among all Jews throughout the world …** (a) **ringleader … he even tried to profane the temple … Then the Jews also joined in the charge** (24.5-9). Paul to Felix: **I cheerfully make my defense** (24.10). To Festus and Agrippa: **I consider myself fortunate** (26.2). He does not sound worried!

Paul would be torn to pieces … an oath neither to eat or drink till they had killed Paul … more than forty of their men are lying in ambush for him (Acts 23.10, 13, 21). A more perilous condition is hard to imagine! He will arrive in Caesarea **cheerful** (24.10), perhaps considering **the two hundred soldiers, with seventy horsemen and two hundred spearmen** (23.23) excessive protection. A compliment! With confidence of acquittal (24.13), Paul once again speaks (not of Jesus, but) of **the resurrection** (23.6; 24.15, 21).

Paul **cheerfully** (Acts 24.10) and with **a clear conscience** (v. 16) defends himself, dismissing the charges against him. At no time was he **disputing with anyone or stirring up a crowd, either in the temple or in the synagogues or in the city** (v. 12). Governor Felix latches on to Paul's claim that witnesses **ought to be here before you** (v. 19; cf. 27.7). So he delays, allowing time to **hear … him speak about faith in Christ Jesus** (v. 24; see v. 25) as **he hoped that money would be given him by Paul** (v. 26). **Felix left Paul in prison** (v. 27).

When two years had elapsed, Felix was succeeded by Porcius Festus (Acts 24.27). The **ambush to kill** (25.3) Paul was still on so the **chief priest and principled men … urged him** (Festus), **asking as a favor** (25. 2, 3) to transport Paul to Jerusalem. Rather, **go down with me to Caesarea** (25.5, 6). Then came Paul's defense (25.8) to their **serious charges** (25.7). Now **Festus, wishing to do the Jews a favor** (25.9) tries to persuade Paul to answer charges in Jerusalem. Jerusalem? **I appeal to Caesar** (25.11), i.e. Nero!

The Jews never abandoned Plan A: **ambush to kill him** (Acts 25.3). That would end these bothersome hearings and toilsome journeys. Paul is unfazed by death threats but not the incarceration, which lingers for two years as Felix was hoping for an extortion gain (24.26). Paul seeks his own release, appealing to Festus just **three days after** (he) **had arrived** (25.1). God gave Paul Roman citizenship and Paul uses this to his advantage. For him, standing trial is the new venue for evangelism (Chapter 26).

Agrippa and Bernice came with great pomp (Acts 25.23)– mostly show, as the role of king by now had little authority. Paul is affirmed. **This man … could have been set free if he had not appealed to Caesar … In a short time you will persuade me to be a Christian** (26.31, 32, 28). Festus, who had kept himself personally detached from the case, now erupts **Paul you are out of your mind** (26.24) **upon hearing Christ … light both to our people and the Gentiles** (26.23).

Herod Agrippa II, an agent of Rome (not Jerusalem), never received local respect and was most unworthy of this **great pomp** (Acts 25.23). Agrippa sides with Rome (and his sisters Bernice and Drusilla and brother in law Felix–see 24.24; 25.23) in the 66-70 A.D. war, subsequent razing of Jerusalem and dispersion the people. He dies at an old age and is sadly remembered for his **would you persuade me** (26.28) question. History compares him poorly with his contemporary Paul.

Paul was brought in … (and) **examined** (Acts 25.25, 26). **I consider myself fortunate** (26.2). **I stand here on trial because of my hope** (26.6). Once **opposing the name of Jesus** (26.9) and **now saying nothing but what the prophets and Moses said would come to pass** (26.22). Could **hope** be a crime? they said to one another, "This man is doing nothing to deserve death and imprisonment … (and) could have been set free if he had not appealed to Caesar" (26.31, 32).

it was decided that we should sail for Italy (Acts 27.1). *We!* Luke did not have to do this! He chooses dangerous travel and an association with a man that could get both of them killed. For Luke and **Aristarchus** (v. 2), providing social and physical support for Paul was a privilege and the will of God. They never looked back. Luke recorded the travel and weather (vv. 7-20). They receive kindness from **Julius ... Publius ... the residents of Malta ...** (and brothers from) **Putteoli ... Appius and Three Taverns** (27.1,3; 28.1, 2, 7, 13-15). Much appreciated (28.15)!

Paul's spectacular life included much (unnecessary) trauma at sea. The **tempestuous wind** (Acts 27.14) ... **storm tossed** (v. 18) was so bad **the sailors were seeking to escape** (v. 30). Every mishap, an opportunity! Paul prophesies (vv. 10, 22, 26). There is no evidence of fear from **standing before Caesar** (v. 24), **running aground** (v. 26), or **striking the reef** (v. 41), which demolished the ship. Wet and cold they **were brought safely** ... (to) **Malta** (28.1). Paul is bit by **a viper** (28.3). Tough times for God's beloved!

Continuing on to Rome, Paul and company receive **unusual kindness** (28.2). **Publius ... received us and entertained us hospitably** (v. 7) ... **honored us** greatly (v. 10) ... **invited to stay** (v. 14). Unexpected blessings! Paul continues his bold ministry: healing the sick (vv. 8, 9) and **call**(ing) **together the local leaders of the Jews** (v. 17) to present his case (which could invite more trouble)! They respond, **we desire to hear from you** ... (and) **in great numbers** (vv. 22, 23)!

The conclusion of Acts of the Apostles comes without a conclusion to Paul's life. He is still in full stride! **From** morning till evening he expounded to them, testifying to the kingdom of God and trying to convince them about Jesus both from the Law of Moses and from the Prophets ... proclaiming the kingdom of God and teaching about the Lord Jesus Christ with all boldness (Acts 28.23, 31), as he had been doing since Cyprus (13.16).

JOHN

John

The prologue to **John** (1.1-18) is also a prologue to life. (1) Life is understood in the framework of eternity (vv. 1, 2), creation (v. 3; cf. v. 10), life's essence (v. 4), and knowledge (vv. 4, 5; cf. v. 9; including **glory ... grace ... truth**–v. 14; cf. vv. 16, 17). There is no better, no other beginning point. (2) The intended application from the prologue: **receive ... believe ...** (and) **become children of God** (v. 12), i.e. enter into a familial relationship with God. **Jesus Christ ... at the Father's side ... has made him known** (vv. 17, 18).

The Gospel of John is the world's greatest evangelistic presentation. Enjoy it! The main issue: Jesus' identity: (1) He is **the Word** (John 1.1, 14), a Greek term. Jesus is Reason personified. (2) He is Creator. **All things were made through him** (v. 3, cf. 10). Jesus accounts for my origin and purpose! (3) **In him was life** (v. 4). Jesus is pure and total life. Everything and everyone else is a pale expression of its fullness.

(4) He **was the light of men ... the true light, which enlightens everyone** (John 1.4, 9). Jesus did not just have it– he *was* it! The needed knowledge, wisdom and truth of God are found in Jesus. Study him to gain knowledge *of him* and knowledge *for life.* This is for **everyone** (v. 9). Of course there is a problem: **darkness** (5)–the antithesis of everything he is and life is. **His own people did not receive him** (v. 11). Chalk up all opposition to *darkness.*

The role of John *the Baptist* is stated twice, **to bear witness about the light** (John 1.7, 8). That will put him in the crosshairs of the authorities. **Who are you? ... What do you say about yourself? ... Why are you baptizing ... ?** (vv. 19, 22, 24). From John comes Jesus' identity (5): one **whose sandal I am not worthy to untie** (v. 27). Both Johns point to the greatness of Jesus. If the evangelistic task is to persuade, let *this* be the subject matter.

(6) Jesus is **full of grace and truth** (John 1.14). This further develops the image of **light** (vv. 4, 8, 9). John next presents a rather deep thought for an introduction: grace and truth is **glory as from the only Son from the Father** (v. 14). **The Word** (vv. 1, 14) is not separate from the Father (vv. 14, 18). As I learn about Jesus from study and experience I must not miss **grace upon grace** (v. 16). I must respond. I **receive him ... believe in his name** (v. 12).

as the prophet Isaiah said (John 1.23). John had been musing in Isaiah (chapters 40, 53) and how it spoke of *him,* **the voice of one crying in the wilderness** (v. 23), and Jesus, (7) **the Lamb of God** (vv. 29, 36). He will **take ... away the sin of the world** (v. 29). Jesus' public ministry is filled with prophetic revelation and dazzle. The apostle John helps me *get* and *stay* on track. Nothing must overshadow divine forgiveness–the work of God. (8) Jesus is **he who baptizes with the Holy Spirit** (v. 33).

Rabbi ... where are you staying? He said to them, "Come and you will see" (John 1.38, 39). **Come and see** (v. 46). **His disciples ... stayed there for a few days** (2.12). The calling of the first disciples featured unstructured, unhurried exposure to Jesus. No special events. No crises. No persuasion. Jesus called them, primarily for *their* sake. They responded because it was right. They were impressed, especially Nathaniel: (9) **You are the Son of God! You are the King of Israel!** (v. 49).

Had John not been careful, his life could have been a tragedy. Those around him saw in him **Christ … Elijah … the Prophet** (John 1.20, 21; cf. v. 25). An opportunist can move ahead in the world, at best becoming a loser; at worst becoming an opponent of God. John was faithful to his calling–a **witness about the light** (v. 8; cf. v. 32), **not worthy … compared to **he who comes after** (v. 27). He baptized Jesus and introduced him, **Behold, the Lamb of God** (v. 35).

Bad news, good news: (1) Though **revealed to Israel … his own people did not receive him** (John 1.31, 11). (2) **two disciples** (of John) … **followed Jesus** (v. 35). Then another (vv. 40-42). Then another (v. 43). Then another (vv. 45-51). More important than the head count was the profound realization of these early converts: **We found the Messiah … We have found him of whom Moses in the Law, and also the prophets wrote … you are the Son of God! You are the King of Israel!** (vv. 41, 45, 49).

The brilliant teaching presented in John 1.35ff is mankind's best first impression of Jesus. (1) Relationships are central. Andrew and John (presumably) asked **where are you staying? He said to them, "Come and you will see."** (1.39). Knowing Jesus for all is a gradual discovery. The **wedding at Cana** was informal learning where he **manifested his glory** (2.1, 11) in a miracle. This section records no heavy teaching; it does include some humor (1.47; 2.4).

(2) **believe** (John 1.50; 2.11, 22) is the operative verb. Jesus wants to know from his first 4 followers, men who apparently were not lacking in commitment, **do you believe?** (1.50). A disciple would have to trust him and **believe ... the Scripture and the word that Jesus had spoken** (2.22). Soon to come: **whoever believes in Him has eternal life** (3.15). Later will come the justification by faith teaching (Galatians 2.16).

On occasion God graciously helps sinners turn to him by revealing signs. If a sign is ever appropriate, it will be in underscoring the presence of Messiah. **the first of his signs** (John 2.11) is turning the water to wine at a wedding (vv. 1-11). A wedding celebration aligned with Jesus' travels. His family is present. With a hint of reluctance (vv. 3-5), Jesus meets a need, extends the joy, **and manifested his glory** (v. 11).

Speaking of signs, John 2.13-22 records Jesus' first disruption of the temple in Jerusalem. Jesus is aggressive, if not violent! Like a prophet, Jesus communicates through actions. **making a whip of cords, he drove them all (money-changers) out of the temple ... overturned their tables** (v. 15). **The Jews said to him, "What sign do you show us ...?"** (v. 18). Jesus relates the temple to his body. Later he will relate his body to the church (see 17.21, 22).

he himself knew what was in man (John 2.25) = Jesus is not about to be impressed by anyone. **Nicodemus** (3.1) was the next to **Come and see** (1.34, 46). In Jesus he saw some form of divinity (3.2), and wanted to learn more, but Jesus quashed that. To **see** (and understand) **the kingdom of God** one needs regeneration (3.3, 7)–more than a good mind. Nicodemus' response shows more charm than puzzlement (v. 4). With an allusion to John (3.5) and his message (see 1.33), Jesus directs Nicodemus to **the Spirit** (3.5, 8) and prophecy fulfillment (3.13, 14).

Nicodemus was inquisitive. Jesus challenges this learned man in his area of strength: theological terms, i.e. **born again** (John 3.3, 7) and **born of the Spirit** (vv. 5, 6, 8). Jesus' analogy ends with a condemnation: **he cannot see the kingdom of God** (v. 3). **Whoever does not believe is condemned already** (v. 18). The religious cannot help but become ruffled. True spirituality is not religiously based. Salvation and eternal life are **heavenly things** (v. 12)– thoroughly spiritual and through Jesus (vv. 16, 18, 36).

Like **the serpent in the wilderness**, Jesus will be **lifted up** (John 3.14)–on the cross, and then in heaven. John's writing frequently uses expressions with more than one meaning (e.g. 2.19). Looking at that bronze serpent (cf. Numbers 21.9) and **believ**(ing) **in him** (v. 16) brings healing and **eternal life** (v. 16). Previous belief was in Jehovah. Now **many believed in his name** (v. 23)! **Believe … in the name of the only Son of God** (v. 18).

The great gospel summary of John 3.16-21 flows from the dialog with Nicodemus (vv. 1-15). Nicodemus receives more information than he bargained for and so does the Bible reader: (1) The gospel is synonymous with **the kingdom of God** (v. 3) and **eternal life** (v. 15). (2) There are no shades of gray. **perish** … be **condemn**(ed) … **or saved** (vv. 16, 17). **light or darkness** (v. 19). **does wicked things** or **does what is true … carried out in God** (vv. 20, 21).

John reveals some things about himself and **the Christ** (John 3.28). John considered his subordinate role as **this joy of mine** (v. 30). He is **sent before him** (v. 28) as a **friend of the bridegroom, who stands and hears him** (v. 29). Jesus' ministry was **given him from heaven** (v. 27), which explains why **all** (were) **going to him. He ... comes from above ...** (and) **is above all ...** (and) **utters the words of God ...** (and) **gives the Spirit without measure** (vv. 31–34).

John the Baptist affirms Jesus for what was **given him from heaven** (John 3.27). This truth gave him **joy ... complete** (v. 29). John **sets his seal to this** (v. 33). The core of vv. 31–36 is **The Father loves the Son and has given all things to his hand** (v. 35). Understand the relationship of the Father and Son before the relationship of the Son with believers–the Father and the Son first; the Son and the world he came to save second. Converts commit to understanding relationships.

Jesus engages **a woman of Samaria** (John 4.7) in the middle of her workday (v. 6). She has a hard exterior. She rebuffs Jesus' request for water (v. 9). He speaks to her of **living water ... a spring of water welling up to eternal life** (vv. 10, 14). She matches wits with him and talks of practicality: (1) he had **nothing to draw water with** (v. 11), and (2) religion–**our father Jacob ... our fathers worshiped on this mountain** (v. 21). Jesus discloses his identity (v. 26) to this woman, who at this point lacks **spirit and truth** (v. 23).

The **woman of Samaria** (John 4.7) carries forward the theme, **Come, see a man** (v. 29; cf. 1.39; 46). (She faithfully *introduces;* no strain to convince.) Jesus had **told** (her) **all she ever did** (v. 29; cf. v. 39). It was all the bad (v. 18). She was not offended and did not recoil, rather, accepted it and accepted Jesus. Conviction is only painful and inciting to the resistant. Evangelism is **food … the will of him** (v. 34).

Jesus continuously makes an impression. **Many Samaritans believed in him because of the woman** (John 4.39). Jesus likens Samaria to **fields white for harvest** (v. 35). Who knew? The disciples are thinking more about Jesus abstaining from a meal. Jesus turns this into a teaching moment: **My food is to do the will of him who sent me and to accomplish his work** (v. 34). I must see this as *my* food as well.

In Samaria, **many more believed because of his word** (John 4.31). Not so in Galilee. **Unless you see signs and wonders you will not believe** (v. 48). Jesus mercifully heals an official's (v. 46) dying **son** (v. 47). Then in Jerusalem he heals **an invalid** (5.5) who was among **a multitude of invalids** (5.3). All marveled at the miracle but it was the subsequent teaching that left the greater impact (5.17-47).

The Jews want to talk about a **Sabbath** violation (John 5.10). Jesus talks about the nature and work of God (vv. 17-47). A greater revelation I can hardly imagine! Jesus–the Son, and his Father are in complete harmony (vv. 18-23, 30) and model unity for the rest of us (v. 29). The **Father** works (v. 19), reveals these works to his **Son** (v. 20), **raises the dead** (v. 21), and is the source of **life** (v. 26). The Son is cued by **the Father** (v. 19) and **judges** on his behalf (v. 22, cf. v. 27). They share honor (v. 26).

Jesus unveiled the unexpected. (Still does!) He heals children (John 4.52). He heals **a multitude** (5.3)–one, an old man sick for a long time (5.5). The **invalid … by the Sheep Gate** (5.5, 2) was a great **sign** (4.53) but **the Jews** (found it) **unlawful** (5.10). *That* is repulsive! Jesus is up for the confrontation: (1) **My Father … is working …and shows him** (the Son) **all that he himself is doing** (5.17, 20). (2) **The Father … has given all judgment to the Son** (5.22).

Witness and testimony are subjects near and dear to Jesus. Self-attestation is not enough (John 5.31). **There is another who bears witness about me** (v. 32). Not just **John** (v. 33) but **the Father** (v. 37). To this add **the works that the Father has given me to accomplish** (v. 36). Also, **You search the Scriptures … it is they that bear witness about me** (v. 39). The Father, John, the works and the Scriptures all point to believ(ing) **the one whom he has sent** (v. 38; cf. vv. 46, 47)!

Little has changed in the battle regarding *belief.* Religious Jews did *not* believe: **If another comes … you will receive him** (John 5.43). Unbelievers **do not have his word … do not believe in the one whom he has sent … do not have the love of God …do not believe his writings** (vv. 38, 42, 47), but they are religious! Christian faith begins with the full acceptance of Jesus' identity. Willing transformation follows. The healings and miracles (**signs**–6.2, 14) hopefully prompt belief.

Jesus uses several core words to describe the reorientation of a follower: (1) **believe** (John 5.38, 44, 46, 47; 6.29, 40) is by far the most common. There are others: (2) **come** (5.40). I must move my body! (3) **look** (6.40). A lengthy focus can burn a lasting impression. (4) **feed … on me** (6.57). **Whoever feeds on my flesh and drinks my blood has eternal life** (v. 54). This is more metaphor than mystery. Linking with Jesus is the only hope for experiencing fullness of life.

they saw the signs that he was doing on the sick (John 6.2). Jesus heals for more reasons than mercy. God was underscoring for the world that Messiah had come *and with signs*. He healed a stranger (5.1-15). He fed followers (6.1-15). He was **walking on the sea** (6.19) before his disciples. 3 categories. 3 dazzling signs. The people want more (6.26) but instead Jesus teaches (6.23-59). The Bread of Life Discourse is deep. Jesus is unconcerned about losing his audience.

The feeding of the 5,000 was the alternative feast in Galilee (see John 5.1) and was quite the **sign** (6.14). Greater was the subsequent and related teaching–the bread of life discourse (6.32-65). I understand unless I am justified by faith I am not saved (Romans 5.1). Here Jesus teaches unless I experience God I am not saved! As bread yields energy, **the bread of life** (John 6.36) yields **life** (v. 53), **eternal life** (v. 40).

Jesus, the teacher, faced monumental obstacles. The people wanted continuous provision (John 6.14, 15, 26). The more theological Jews had bones to pick (v. 41). Jesus had given them an **I am** (v. 35) divinity link and boldly promised **whoever comes to me shall not hunger, and whoever believes in me shall never thirst … never** (to be) **cast out** (v. 35). Whoever **believes in him … feeds on** him (vv. 40, 57) **abides in** (him) **and I in him** (v. 56). This is a work of **the spirit … the flesh is no help at all** (v. 63).

Jesus continues teaching about the work of God (see John 4.34). **This is the work of God, that you believe in Him whom he has sent** (John 6.29). Jesus says *work*. The Jews think *signs* (v. 30). Jesus links the sign of manna (which provided physical sustenance) with believing in him, **the bread of life** (v. 35), resulting in **eternal life** (v. 40). If not starting from belief, there are no works of God of any consequence. The Jews reject his self-exaltation (vv. 41, 42) and miss his metaphor (vv. 48-59).

eat the flesh of the Son of Man and drink his blood (John 6.52)–a metaphor, not a sacrament (see 10.6a), similar to Jesus' words to Nicodemus, *You must be born again (3.7),* and to the woman, *whoever drinks of the water that I will give him will never be thirsty again (4.13).* More than **the loaves** (6.11, 12), Jesus is sustenance. Beyond that, Jesus refers to the atonement–**my blood** (6.55, 56). The result is **life** (6. 53, 54; cf. vv. 56-58)–life *in Christ* (Paul's formulation).

This is a hard saying, who can listen to it? ... After this many of his disciples turned back and no longer walked with him (John 6.60, 66). So close. Two observations: (1) Natural disposition does not incline one to seek a holy God (7.5). When challenged to think ... and repent, **his disciples were grumbling** (7.51), naturally! (2) Humans are responsible but God has final say. **no one can come to me unless it is granted him by the Father** (6.65, cf. v. 44).

People **grumbled** (John 6.41, 61), disbelieved (7.5), accused him of **leading the people astray** (7.12), and **were muttering** (7.12, 32). The atmosphere was tense. **no one spoke openly of him** (7.13). **you seek to kill me** (7.19). Jesus is teaching his favorite subject: himself! He is the one sent by the Father. *Sent* is referred to 21x in chapters 5-8. **He who sent me is true** (7.28). Compliance with the will of the Father meant everything to Jesus–a desire that reflects his divinity and humanity!

John 6 & 7: good news and bad news; salvation and rejection; mounting tension. People were **grumbling ... muttering** (6.61; 7.12, 32). People **walked with ... believed** (6.66; 69; 7.31)–good news, and did **not** (7.5)–bad. Why? Jesus keeps the subject on himself– **the Son of Man** (6.62) sent by **the living Father** (6.57). For this, and in spite of his **learning** (7.15) and the healing ministry (7.23), people wanted Jesus **kill**(ed) (7.20, 25). Stunning teaching (7.37-39) results in discord (7.40-52).

It was **the last day of the feast, the great day** (John 7.37). Jesus had been ramping up his teaching ministry. Hostilities were increasing. The crescendo turns out to be an invitation: **Jesus cried out ... If anyone is thirsty let him come to me and drink ... he said this about the Spirit** (7.37-39). He looks past the cross and Pentecost (7.39) to the great on going experience of life awaiting **those who believe in him** (7.39). The ministry of the Holy Spirit is satisfying and life changing.

Jesus continues to proclaim (1) himself: **the Father ... sent me ... I am from above ... I ... speak just as the Father taught me** (John 8.16, 23, 28). Here that teaching is to **the Jews who had believed ...** (and) **not believe**(d) (vv. 31, 46) and includes (2) a primer on sin. **you will die in your sin. Where I am going** (heaven) **you cannot come ...** The reason why you do not hear them (the words of God) is that you are not of God (vv. 21, 47; cf. v. 24).

(3) The gospel call: **be free indeed ... love me ... keep ... my word** (John 8.36, 42, 51, 52; cf. v. 31). Jesus alludes to his death, the atonement, but it is veiled (v. 22). He was among those who would hasten that day (vv. 37, 59). Jesus' teachings about himself, sin and the gospel result not in wonder and inquisitiveness but in ire, rejection and insult– **Now we know that you have a demon!** (v. 52; cf. v. 48). Now a mob, they attempt execution (v. 58).

Whoever follows me ... will have the light of life (John 8.12)! *Follow* implies a walk. As I follow Jesus, my life consists of actions that reflect truth and embody life. Life is grounded on his teachings. Jesus goes on to embellish: **the Father who sent me bears witness about me ... I am from above. You are of this world; I am not of this world** (vv. 16, 23). Again, the teaching is about himself and his Father. The center of truth and wisdom is *Christology!* Other alternatives are inadequate.

The stakes are high! **Unless you believe I am he you will die in your sins. So they said to him, "Who are you?"** (John 8.24). Contention. Jesus: **You cannot bear to hear my word. You are of your father the devil ... you are not of God** (vv. 43, 44). The Jews: **So they picked up stones to throw at him** (v. 59). A high view of Christ provokes every other ideology resulting in confrontation and anger. Interfaith congeniality will only go so far.

After this ... But after ... About the middle of ... On the last day ... When they heard ... Again ... As he passed by

107

(John 7.1, 10, 14, 37, 40; 8.12; 9.1). Jesus' life is presented as a *packed narrative,* similar to the writing style of Mark (especially Mark 1, 2). Followers of Jesus take note: With kingdom of God eyes, each day can be a string of events, interactions and initiatives for Jesus' sake and on his behalf, scaled down of course, but significant. See Matthew 5.13-16 and make life a *packed narrative.*

Death threats (John 8.59), **division** (9.16) and dis**belief** (9.18) are followed with intensive teaching. Once again, Jesus teaches about himself. **I am the door ... enter by me ...** (and) **be saved** (10.9). What makes him this lone door? **I lay down my life for the sheep** (including) ... **other sheep that are not of this fold** (10.16). Not only that but he will **take it up again** (10.17, 18)! Atonement and resurrection! The great result: **one flock** (10.16)!

And his disciples asked him, "Rabbi, who sinned, this man or his parents ... ?" (John 9.2). The disciples bring up a topic Jesus had recently spoken about (see 8.34, 46). Infirmity is not punishment for sin (v. 3), rather **that the works of God might be displayed in him** (v. 3). Jesus is **the light of the world** (v. 5). **while it is day ... we must work** (v. 4). Mercifully, the man is given sight, but only after a walk to **the pool of Siloam** (v. 7). Another sign; another instance of Jesus doing the unexpected.

John 9.7-34 contains no quotations from Jesus. It is a dialogue between the Pharisees, other Jews and a beggar. To align with Jesus is **to be put out of the synagogue** (v. 22). Ostracization–which happened (v. 34)! The people are confused, if not torn: **He does not keep the Sabbath** and

How can a man who is a sinner do such signs? ... **This is an amazing thing!** (vv. 16, 30). Jesus is revealed not only as a prophet (v. 17), but as the Daniel 7 **Son of Man** (v. 35; cf. 13.31)!

Are we also blind? (John 9.40). They were! Making a case that they were not would only maximize the guilt (9.41). More metaphors: They were deaf, because the real **sheep hear his voice** (10.3). That would make Jesus **the good shepherd** (10.11). **I lay down my life for the sheep** (10.15, also vv. 16-18). But he is also **the door of the sheep** (10.7). **If anyone enters by me he will be saved ... and find pasture** (10.9). To the opposition these are **words of one who is oppressed by a demon** (10.21).

It was winter and the temple confrontation **At the time** (of) **the Feast of Dedication** (John 10.22) had a frosty tone! **tell us plainly** (v. 24). Jesus, initially not answering their question, is plenty clear: **you are not part of my flock** (v. 26). Then the fullest of disclosures: **I and the Father are one** (v. 30) = **God** (v. 33; cf. v. 38). Jesus pleads with them to consider **The works that I do** (v. 25; cf. vv. 31, 33, 37). **The Jews picked up stones again ... sought to arrest him** (vv. 31, 39; cf. 11.9, 52, 57).

I have shown you many good works from the Father (John 10.31). Verses 22-38 link Jesus to his works and to the Father. This is not theological minutia! Jesus boasts, **I and the Father are one** (10.30)–a precious familial profession. Jesus credits his works as **the works of my Father** (10.37)–to Him be the glory (13.31). This prompts a **division** (10.19) and attempts to **stone him** (10.31) and **arrest him** (10.39). But **many believed in him there** (10.41)!

John 11.1-44, close to the halfway point in the gospel, records a resurrection–of Lazarus. From the start Jesus knew his sick friend would die and that he would raise him (v. 4). (1) Jesus taught, **I am the resurrection and the life. Whoever believes in me, though he die, yet shall he live** (v. 25). (2) **Jesus wept** (v. 35). Why? As one who also came **to console (Martha and Mary) concerning their brother** (v. 19), Jesus shares their grief–part of the human experience.

The illness … is for the glory of God (John 11.4). Followers of Christ, unlike **Thomas** (v. 16), maintain a positive perspective **so that the Son of God may be glorified** (v. 4) first, to get *a new lease on life* second. The clear focus of chapter 11 is God's glory: He / Jesus (1) **love**(s) (v. 3); (2) teaches (vv. 9, 10, 25, 26); (3) weeps (vv. 33–35); (4) prays (vv. 41, 42); (5) heals (v. 43); (6) retreats **with the disciples** (v. 54; cf. 12.2).

Jesus' signs were interpreted as opposition (John 11.45-47). Therefore a resurrection would be over the top! Plotting commenced (v. 57). Clueless Caiaphas unknowingly speaks a truth he did not intend (v. 50). Jesus' death would not appease Romans; it would propitiate holy wrath and expiate sin (see Romans 3.25; 1 John 2.2). Jesus' death would **gather into one the children of God who are scattered abroad** (v. 52). But not yet. **Jesus went from there to the region near the wilderness** (v. 54).

Jesus returned to Bethany for another dinner served by Martha, sister of Lazarus and Mary (John 12.1-7). Lazarus by now had celebrity status (vv. 9, 10)! Again, there are complaints. Earlier (see Luke 10.38ff) it was Martha, provider of a fine meal, who did not appreciate Mary's focus on Jesus. Now it is Judas who saw **three hundred denarii** (v. 5) worth of perfume poured on Jesus by Mary. The **thief** (v. 6) charges the worshiper with misconduct! **Jesus said, "Leave her alone ... "** (v. 7).

Some Greeks ... wish(ed) **to see Jesus** (John 12.20, 21). Now was not the time. Jesus is pondering his death. He was **to be glorified** (v. 23), dying like a **grain of wheat fall**(ing) **to the earth** (v. 24). **glorify** (vv. 23, 28) is the chosen descriptive word, reinforced by **a voice ... from heaven** (v. 28). Both Jesus (11.42), and **This voice** (12.30) speak for the sake of the listener–not an exercise of self-expression. Jesus wants us to understand *glory,* as the Father does.

many of the Jews were going away believing in Jesus ... they still did not believe in him (John 12.11, 37). Undeniable events and wisdom are received, except for those religiously predisposed. That was the reason for the v. 37 unbelief. The words of Jesus polarize: **if it dies it bears much fruit ... now is the judgment of this world ... when I am lifted up I will draw all people to myself ... the one who walks in darkness does not know where he is going** (vv. 24, 31, 32, 35).

John / Jesus does not make *belief* easy to understand: **they still did not believe ... they could not believe ... many even of the authorities believed ... whoever believes** (John 12.37, 39, 42, 46). The will to believe is not beyond God's sovereignty (see 6.64, 65). Far, far from just assent, belief is (1) accepting **authority** ... (from) **the Father** (v. 49; cf. v. 44); (2) **receiv**(ing Jesus') **words** (v. 48) as **light** (v. 46). True believers do not turn back.

I am not to pin just one meaning to *belief*–the primary verb in the gospel of John. For some *belief* was a solid and saving commitment (John 11.25-27). For others it was just a favorable inclination. **many even of the authorities believed in him, but for fear of the Pharisees, they did not confess it** (12.42). Belief in Jesus occurs through the permission of the Father (12.40, cf. 6.44) and is tantamount to believing in **the Father**–a truth Jesus explains at length (vv. 44-50).

Against a dark background, John 13 reveals great truths as events and emotions collide. **Jesus ... had come from God and was going back** (v. 3). This comforting hope was disturbed by the presence of **the devil** ... (through) **Judas** (v. 2; also, vv. 19, 21-30), then his foreknowledge of Peter's denial (vv. 36-38). Jesus could have taken some personal time but instead **washed their feet** (v. 12) with an accompanying teaching (vv. 14-19). Then the **new commandment ... love one another** (v. 34).

having loved his own who were in the world, he loved them to the end ... A new commandment I give you that you love one another (John 13.1, 34). The context is foot washing. Love for one another is manifested in self-effacing service. Modeled by the **Lord and Teacher** (v. 14), no one will claim exemption. And there is no one disqualified from receiving esteeming acts of love. The simple logic behind service: **just**

as I have loved you (v. 34). Profound results: **all people will know that you are my disciples** (v. 35).

Jesus links love with **glory** (John 13.31, 32: 12.23, 28). Jesus' ordeal on the cross is the ultimate expression of love–and glory! My job is to see this and appreciate it as did Jesus and **the Father who sent** him (12.49). The disciples had trouble with this. The cross would also mark the end of their relationship with Jesus as they knew it. **You will seek me ... you cannot follow me now** (13.33, 36). There will be coming a great distance between Peter and Jesus (v. 38).

I go and prepare a place for you (John 14.3) = I now can claim the hope Jesus had! See 13.3. But I need not hasten that day for to know Jesus is to already know **God** (v. 1) and the **Father** (vv. 6, 7, 9-11), which brings me back again to the imperatives: **Believe me ... believe ... the works** (vv. 11, 12). Then **do the works** (v. 12)! Then **pray, ask in my name** (v. 13). **love me ... keep my commandments** (v. 15). Believing goes beyond mental exercise!

Jesus reveals the problem (John 13.33) and then the good news for **afterward** (13.36). **I go to prepare a place for you. I will come again and will take you to myself** (14.2, 3). Peter, Thomas and Philip (13.36; 14.5, 8) still were not understanding Jesus, who does not give detailed explanations. Instead he points to his own greatness and primacy (14.6, 7, 10-14). **Believe** (14.11, 12)–3x. Then, **greater works than these will he do, because I am going to the Father** (14.12).

There is suppose to be no such thing as a stupid question but 3 of the disciples submit entries: (1) Thomas: **How can we know the way? Jesus said to him, "I am the way..."** (John 14.5, 6). Thomas already had been told **the way** ... (Jesus is) **going** (v. 4), i.e. to the cross (14.37; 12.32), to the Father (13.1; also 14.28). Like **Simon Peter** (13.36), Thomas misses the main point–the main attraction–Jesus, himself! *He* is the way, more than any itinerary!

(2) A question phrased as a statement. From Philip: **Lord, show us the Father** (John 14.8) *The Father* has been the focus of Jesus' teaching with about 60 references in chapters 1-13. An exasperated Jesus responds, **Have I been with you so long and you do not know me, Philip?** (v. 9). Jesus' character, actions and teaching represent the most complete description of the eternal, creator, redeemer God as we are going to get!

(3) **Judas (not Iscariot) said to him, "Lord, How is it that your will manifest yourself to us and not to the world?"** (John 14.22). Jesus responds, **keep my words** (vv. 23, 24). Jesus rephrases his teaching in vv. 10, 12, 15 and 21. The world has received ample exposure to Jesus and this exposure continues as his followers obey. I am to put more energy into obedience than question asking. The Father and the Son promise to **come to him and make our home with him** (v.23), i.e. he who keeps his words.

the Father who dwells in me does his works (John 14.10). This begins (or re-starts) Jesus teaching on works, obedience and **keep**(ing) **the commandments** (v. 15). When fulfilled, Jesus promises to **manifest** (him)**self** (v. 21). Wow! Because his followers want to *get this right,* Jesus sends the Holy Spirit to **bring to remembrance all that I have said to you** (v. 26). Many thanks! My obedience is the first purpose of the Helper / Holy Spirit (v. 31)! Then comes **peace** (v. 27).

the Father ... will give you another Helper (John 14.15). This blockbuster revelation had already been hinted to (7.39). He said **I am going** (14.12), now, **I will come** (14.28)! **The Helper (will) be with you forever ... and will be in you** (14. 16, 17)–**the Helper, the Holy Spirit, whom the Father will send in my name** (14.26). For those who **love me ... and keep my words** (14.24), there is **peace** (14.27).

The John 14-17 discourse refers to the Father 48 times. = I am to think of him and credit him. **Bear**(ing) **much fruit** (John 15.5) is an aspect of and a result of **keep**(ing) **my commandments ... keep**(ing) **my words** (14.15, 24). Bearing fruit requires pruning from the Father–vinedresser (15.1, 2) and abiding in Christ (15.4, 5, 6, 7). I accept the continuum that connects my obedience *to* my private life with God, and *to* God's work in the world.

The theme of love is prominent–from the foot washing to Calvary. Jesus repeats his 13.34, 35 command: **This is my commandment, that you love one another as I have loved you** (John 15.12). Toward the ends of loving deeds and bearing fruit, **ask the Father in my name, (and) he may give it to you** (15.16). Again, **Ask and you will receive** (16.24). God promises to endorse and support efforts to bring glory to the Father and his Son.

Choose the greater threat from John 15: (1) not **bear**(ing) **fruit** (v.2; cf. vv. 4, 6, 7); not **abid**(ing) **in me** (v. 6; cf. vv. 4,

5); or (2) hatred and persecution from the world (vv. 16-25). If it is (1), I will **abide in** ... (Jesus') **words** (v. 7), **ask of the Father** toward bearing fruit (16.23,24), and **keep** ... (his) **commandments** (v. 10). Then my **joy may be full** (v. 11) and I will be **called** (Jesus') **friend** (v. 15)! Jesus: **so I have loved you. Abide in my love** (v. 9).

Jesus promises peace, joy, love and his intervention during times of trouble (John 14.27; 15.11, 12, 16). I need it and will need it! **you are not of this world ... therefore the world hates you ... If they persecuted me, they will also persecute you** (15.19, 20). **they have seen and hated both me and my Father ... without a cause** (15.24, 25). Jesus addresses the special enmity evil has with truth (16.3). We expect conflict until we **see** him (16.22).

With Jesus' departure, the Holy Spirit fills the vast void. **it is to your advantage that I go away** (John 16.7). **the Spirit of truth ... will guide you into all the truth** (16.13). The Holy Spirit serves by (1) underscoring the *truth* (14.26; 15.26; 16.14) and by (2) **convict**(ing) **the world concerning sin and righteousness and judgment** (16.8). Jesus said this is how **he will glorify me** (16.14). Come Holy Spirit and align us to your truth!

He will glorify me (John 16.14) was stated as Jesus had been magnifying the Holy Spirit! That Spirit is **from the Father ...** (and) **of truth** (15.26). Herein lies the foundation of Christian spirituality: **he will convict** (16.8) and **guide** (16.13) and **take what is mine and declare it to you** (16.15), i.e. the ministry of Jesus continues even though we **will not see** (16.19) him. **that your joy may be full** (16.24)!

Now you are speaking plainly (John 16.29). Plain you want? Plain you get, but it is not going to be pleasant: **you will be scattered ... and leave me alone** (16.32). Correction: **yet I am not alone, for my Father is with me** (16.32). Jesus continues his discourse with more about his Father and their relationship with his chapter 17 prayer. Jesus **accomplished the work** (17.5) his Father gave him to do by **manifest**(ing his) **name to the people** (17.6).

the hour is coming, indeed it has come (John 16.32). Hell is about to break loose yet Jesus has been given **authority over all flesh** (17.2). *Wow!* No act of evil gets past our sovereign God. He has a plan for salvation and will fulfill it! With the cross ahead, Jesus is comforted **for I have given them the words that you gave me, and they have received them** (17.8). He is including his followers (and me) in this holy communion! **I am praying for them ... I am glorified in them ... keep them in your name** (17.9-11). Another *wow!*

Jesus described the church as **the people ... you gave me out of the world** (John 17.6). **They have kept your word ... they believe that you sent me ... they may have my joy fulfilled in themselves ... they are not of this world ... that ... love ... may be in them** (vv. 6, 8, 13, 16, 26). Obedience, faith, joy, separation and love are the marks of the church that produce genuine unity and effective evangelism (vv. 22, 23).

I am glorified in them. And I am no longer in the world (John 17.10, 11). I must never underestimate Jesus' love and care for this one segment of society. **for their sake I consecrate myself** (v. 19). **that they might have my joy ... They are not of this world** (vv. 13, 16). Why? **I have given**

them your word ... your word is truth ... Sanctify them in the truth (vv. 14, 17; cf. v. 19) **that they may become perfectly one** (v. 23). In this way **glory** ... (is) **given to them** (v. 22).

soldiers and some officers (John 18.3) came to arrest Jesus. Jesus yields: **I am he** (vv. 5, 6, 8). With that simple declaration, and because of who said it, **they drew back and fell to the ground** (v. 6). God's agenda is overriding man's. Always! **Peter**'s resistance had little significance (v. 10). The Jews, like **Caiaphas** (v. 14), had no idea they were fulfilling prophecy (v. 32) in seeking a Roman execution. Annas, Caiaphas and Pilate held no animus against Jesus but were nonetheless pawns in this evil plot.

Jesus gives himself up. **I am he** (John 18.5, 6, 7). He is ready. **Shall I not drink the cup ... ?** (v. 11)–the cup of God's wrath (cf. Isaiah 51.17, Revelation 14.10). Jesus begins a parade from one person of authority to another (v. 13). Actually, they are pipsqueaks from the perspective of God's kingdom– the only perspective that matters. **The high priest then questioned Jesus** (v. 19)–just going through the motions. None of Annas' questions merited a response from the Teacher (vv. 20-22).

Even less for Caiaphas. **Annas then sent him bound to Caiaphas ... they led Jesus from the house of Caiaphas** (John 18.24, 28). Nothing memorable took place there. Next up, **Pilate** who is not impressed with the limp charges (vv. 29-32). He probes the insurrection possibility, **Are you the King of the Jews?** (v. 33). Then, **What is truth?** (v. 38). All a sorry bunch of questioners. Meanwhile, evil kicks into high gear. Jesus is beaten again and again (18.22; 19.1-3).

...even **Pilate** (John 18.29-19.22), symbol of Roman authority (and taxes)! His 10 years in Judea with the defiant Jews were marked with frequent altercations. To him Jesus was never a threat. The oft unmanagable Jews were. **I find no guilt in him** (18.38; 19.6). The Jews feigned allegiance (19.15) **So he delivered him over to them to be crucified** (19.16). Pilate moved on as he had arrived: important in the darkened world, but a colossal failure for eternity. Philo recorded his eventual suicide.

Crucify him, crucify him! (John 19.6). Pilate does not want to go through with it (vv. 6-13). Jesus puts Pilate in his place regarding true **authority** (vv. 10, 11)! Pilate acquiesces to the shouting crowd (v. 16). The **inscription ... on the cross ... in Aramaic, in Latin and in Greek** (v. 20) is his symbolic protest to the crowd and his own decision. Very sorry diplomacy! Ignominy best describes the way Jesus is condemned.

the tunic was seamless ... myrrh and aloes, about seventy-five pounds in weight ... a new tomb ... the stone had been taken away (John 19.23, 39, 41; 20.1). Jesus wore not an ordinary tunic. He received the appropriate burial, and in an upscale tomb, with an uncommon round stone—evidence of luxury at the scene of his death and burial! What are we to do with our possessions if not glorify God with them? Only a **Judas** would consider this a waste (cf. 12.3-5).

Mary the student (see Luke 10.39) had more to learn about Jesus. She **came to the tomb ... weeping** (John 20.1, 11)

119

looking for the dead Jesus. **They have taken my Lord, and I do not know where they have laid him** (vv. 2, 13). **She ... saw Jesus standing** (v. 14; cf. vv. 19, 26; 21.4). **go to my brothers and say to them ...** (v. 17). Jesus to the 11: **I am sending you** (v. 21). Mary is not called to *contemplation* but *action!*

John was **the other disciple, the one whom Jesus loved** (John 20.2; cf. 18.16; 20.3, 4, 8)–the identity he preferred. John was profoundly affected by Jesus' warm, personal love (phileo). He cannot contain the fact that he was the first *to get it,* **he saw and believed** (v. 8). Mary suspected a body snatcher; Peter needed more time. John **believed ... that he must rise from the dead** (vv. 8, 9)–the first truth to be embraced by any disciple!

Faith rests upon evidence. **I have seen the Lord** (John 20.18). **He showed them his hands and his side** (v. 20). **We have seen the Lord** (v. 25). **Put your finger here and see my hands** (v. 27). **Simon Peter heard that it was the Lord** (21.7). Christianity welcomes and pursues the empirical evidence, amply provided by God. Christians loathe fideism. **Jesus did many other signs** (20.30)–many reasons to believe the foundation of our faith is solid.

Jesus **stood among them** (John 20.19, 26) to bless them. He delivers the message, **Peace be with you** (20.19, 21). He gives them a taste of **the Holy Spirit** (20.22). He helps them with *their* specialty, **fishing** (21.3-10)! He said, **Come and have breakfast** (21.12). At the same time Jesus was / is a bit unfamiliar. Mary **thought him to be the gardener** (20.15). **on the shore ... the disciples did not know that it was Jesus**

(21.4). **none ... asked ... who are you?** (21.12). Knowing Jesus conjoins relationship, blessing and mystery.

Jesus did many other signs in the presence of his disciples, which are not written (John 20.30). But John has one more story to tell–about Peter's **haul ... of large fish** (21.11). After receiving the great commission (20.21) **Peter said ... I am going fishing** (21.3), probably needing some time and help **believing** (20.31). If Peter is typical, spiritual growth is slow. Teaching received (20.15-19) results in growth. Again, it is slow (21.21).

Jesus loves to confront, challenge and teach. He gives Peter three opportunities to confess his love (John 21.15-18), which Peter does. Peter's commission to **feed my lambs ... tend my sheep ... feed my sheep** (vv. 15-17) has become the rubric of Christian ministry. Who of us is *not* charged to teach and care for others, to one extent or another? Horizontal comparisons are not appropriate (vv. 20-22). *Phileo* and *agape* love are delivered through believers who extend the influence of the ever present, but otherwise unseen Jesus.

John's great contribution, penned at an old age, ends where it began. **Were every one of them (... other things that Jesus did ...) written, I suppose that the world itself could not contain the books** (John 21.25). The Word from heaven (1.1, 14) is truth and has an immeasurable supply of life. Followers have an eternity to explore and absorb, starting now, and not in drips and drabs. The more I receive, the more opportunity to be **bearing witness about these things** (v. 24). To God be the glory!

1 John

Two featured words as John opens his letter: (1) Manifest. **the word of life ... was manifest ... the Father was made manifest ... we have seen and heard** (1 John 1.1-3). The central items God wants to reveal, *he has!* (2) Fellowship. This manifestation, **fellowship with the Father** (v. 4), is the center of Christian fellowship, which in turn makes **our joy ... complete** (v. 4). Our fellowship comes from **walking in the light** knowing we are **cleansed from ... all sin** (v. 7).

I am writing to you, and close variations of this phrase are repeated 8x (1 John 2.1-14). John seems to be motivated more by the recipients than by his desire to write. **to you =** for you: **so that you may not sin** (v. 1); **because your sins are forgiven** (v. 12); **because you know him** (v. 13); **because you have overcome the evil one** (v. 13); **because you are strong and the Word of God abides in you** (v. 14). So we all now have the resources for success!

There is no virtue in fideism. Faith rests upon facts. John does not make faith pronouncements until he first establishes empirical evidences. First, consider what **we have heard ... seen ... touched ... made manifest** (1 John 1.1-2). For us today, this is a directive to examine the historicity and evidences of the resurrection. It is because of *that* we can believe **the blood of Jesus his Son cleanses us from all sin** (v. 7). We then **walk in the light** (v. 7)!

God is light (1 John 1.5) and in that light **life was made manifest** (v. 2) in **the word of life** (v. 1). Without light and life **we walk in darkness … and do not practice the truth … the truth is not in us** (v. 6). Those in darkness deny it (1.6, 8; 2.4). And then they are denied **fellowship with us … with one another … with the Father and with his Son Jesus Christ** (vv. 3, 7)! So **we confess our sins** … (for) **the blood of Jesus his Son cleanses us from all our sin** (vv. 9, 7). He is the propitiation for our sins (2.2, cf. 2.12)!

if we walk in the light, as he is in the light (1 John 1.7), **we keep his commandments** (2.3), i.e. obey, and **love** (2.10). Obedience and love are intertwined. In obedience, **keep**(ing) **his word … the love of God is perfected** (2.5). **whoever hates … darkness has blinded his eyes** (2.11) and darkness is manifest in **love** (for) **the world or the things of the world … the desires of the flesh and the desires of the eyes and the pride of possessions** (2.15, 16).

Victims of spiritual warfare can become threats to the church. Some **went out from us because they were not of us** (1 John 2.19). This hurts because when **they** were with us, they were friends. But they had bad core beliefs–in this case they **denie**(d) **the Father and the Son** (v. 22) and needed to go, lest bad teaching infest the whole. **No one who denies the Son has the Father** (v. 23). Many deny the Son but profess a relationship with the Father. Never the case!

Perils and problems: (1) **the world** (1 John 2.15-17)– temporary, **passing away** (v. 17); (2) **antichrist … antichrists** (v. 18) and their ilk–those who **den**(y) **the Father and the Son … that Jesus is the Christ** (v. 22); (3) **those who are trying to** deceive (v. 26). Assuming a sound base, **Let what you heard from the beginning abide in you** (v. 24). **practice righteousness** (v. 29) and look forward to the eternal state (2.25-3.3).

John's teaching on sin: (1) **Do not** (I John 2.15; cf.1, 4, 6)! (2) View Jesus as the key to victory (2.1, 2, 12, 29; 3.5). (3) **darkness … lawlessness** (2.8; 3.4) **does not keep his commandments** (2.5). (4) Sin is furthered by **the devil** (3.8; cf. 2.13) and **antichrist** (2.18) who lie, **den(y) Jesus is the Christ** (2.22) and **deceive** (2.26; 3.7). (5) The antithesis of sin is **light** (2.9), **love** (2.15; 3.14) and **righteousness** (3.7).

60 years or so after John received from Jesus, "Go into all *the world…*" (Mark 16.15), *the world*, if anything, was an even greater force to overcome. **Do not love the world …** (it) **is not from the Father …** (and) **is passing away** (1 John 2.15-17). **the world does not know us** (3.1). John had not given up on the mission field. His eyes were open to see it as a great contaminant. So if the world **did not know him** (3.1), how could its value system have any attraction to me?

love (1 John 3.1-3; 11-24; 4.7-21). **the Father has given** (it) **to us** (3.1; cf. 4.7). **We know we have passed out of darkness into life, because we love … in deed and in truth** (3.14, 18; cf. 3. 16, 17), with the reference point **he loved us and sent his Son to be the propitiation of our sins** (4.10). **whoever loves has been born of God** (4.7). **he has given us his Spirit** (4.13) and so **there is no fear in love** (4.18). **whoever abides in love … (has) confidence for the day of judgment** (4.16, 17).

You know and **we know** are repeated sentence starters (1 John 3.5, 14, 16, 19). **you all have knowledge** (2.20). Needed reminders: **You know ... he appeared to take away sin** (3.5) ... **we have passed out of death into life** (3.14) ... **love, that he laid down his life for us** (3.16) ... **that we are of the truth** (3.19). These are among the basic truths that assure God-centeredness and the subsequent victory.

lawlessness ... the practice of sinning ... the devil (1 John 3.4, 8) are all anathema to **one born of God** (3.9; cf. 3.6). So **he cannot keep sinning because he has been born of God** (3.9). **You know that he** (Jesus) **appeared to take away sins ... to destroy the works of the devil** (3.5, 8). Count on **the spirit of antichrist ... and the spirit of error** (4.3, 6) to challenge this as well as the nature of **Jesus Christ ... from God ... come in the flesh** (4.2, 3).

do not believe every spirit, but test the spirits (1 John 4.1). Spiritual warfare goes beyond the battlefield of emotion (fear, anxiety and depression). Look to false teachers, **false prophets** (v. 1) and **the spirit of error** (v. 6). **the spirit of the antichrist** (v. 3) has a bad message and **the world listens** (v. 5). The first target of the evil spirit is the mind, *then* the emotions. **know the spirit of truth** (v. 6).

see whether they are from God (1 John 4.1). **test** (v. 1): Do they **not confess Jesus** (v. 2)? Do they **not listen to us** (v. 6)? I know I am passing the test when I **overcome** (v. 4; cf. 5.3). For sure, this is just general instruction but I get the point: Christianity has a doctrine of separation. And **Whoever knows God ...** (will) **know the Spirit of Truth and spirit of error** (v. 6). Those who don't just **keep on sinning** (5.18).

1 John 4 is the chapter on light (vv. 1-6) and then love (vv. 7-21). We **love one another, for love is from God** (v. 7). He is the reason (**the propitiation for our sins** – v. 10). He is the source (**not that we have loved God but that he loved us** – v. 10). **God is love** (and we) … **abide in God** (v. 16). The result: an absence of **fear** (v. 18), **hate** (v. 20) and disobedience (5.2-4). We all work out the lingering evidences of sin (1.8; 5.16-18).

God sent his only Son into the world, so that we might live through him (1 John 4.9). There are many dynamics in a full life but in 1 John 4.7-5.2 there is one–love. **Let us love one another for love is from God** (v. 7). **this is love … that he loved us** (v. 10). To be more specific, he **sent his Son to be a propitiation for our sins** (v. 10). Jesus set the standard. **if God so loved us, we also ought to love one another** (v. 11). **whoever abides in love, abides in God** (v. 16).

We practice righteousness … we love and obey his commandments … everyone who has been born of God overcomes the world (1 John 3.10; 5.2, 4). Confident. Uncomplicated. Christ makes it so and grants ability to **Whoever believes in the Son of God** (v. 10)! **And this is the victory that has overcome the world—our faith** (5.4). **Whoever has the Son has life** (5.12). **believe in the name of the Son of God** (5.13).

1 John 5 presents John at his unpredictable and inconsistent best (especially vv. 8-9; 16-21) but 5.1-6 flows logically: **Everyone who loves the Father loves … For this is the love of God, that we keep his commandments** (1 John 5.1, 2). The one who believes Jesus is the one who loves and then obeys.

Regeneration leads to faith which leads to love which leads to obedience which leads to **overcom**(ing) **the world** (v. 5).

There is sin that leads to death (1 John 5.16). What is it? Be content with the explanation in v. 18: **everyone who has been born of God does not keep on sinning.** Continuous, habitual neglect and disobedience does not **overcome the world** (v. 5) and **leads to death** (v. 16). John has been addressing the sin problem since chapter one and he ends with it: **Little children, keep yourself from idols** (v. 21).

2 John

truth and love (2 John 3) are the dominant themes of this short letter. *Truth:* **walking in truth** (v. 4; cf. 3 John 4) is what **many deceivers** (v. 7) failed to do–not **abid**(ing) **in the teaching of Christ** (v. 9). *Love:* **And this is love that you walk according to the commandments** (v. 6; cf.1 John 5.3). **love one another** (v. 5). Love is why John **hope**(d) **to come ... and talk face to face** (v. 12; cf. 3 John 13), rather than write.

love one another ... do not receive him into your house or give him a greeting (2 John 5, 10). A disconnect? Both actions flow from **truth**, referred to 5x in vss. 1-4. **love ... Grace mercy and peace ... joy** (vv. 1, 3, 12) flow through the truth–truth distorted by **many deceivers** (v. 7) who cut away at the person and **teaching of Christ** (v. 9). Pass this along to those we **love in truth** (v. 1).

3 John

I must never think of church as an institution. That will miss the main point, which is relationships. John writes a letter to **whom** (he) **loved** (3 John 1). He commends **Gaius** (v. 1) for the hospitality shown to **the brothers** (vv. 3, 5) and scorns **Diotrophes** for **refus**(ing) **to welcome the brothers** (v. 10). (Diotrophes had an **authority** (v. 9) problem!) Relationships: **The friends greet you. Greet the friends, every one of them** (v. 15).

Diotrophes was a small man who **put himself first** and did not **acknowledge ... authority** (3 John 9). Rather than pull rank, John details the indictment against him (vv. 9-11). Diotrophes is a controlling leader who **stops those who want to ... welcome the brothers ... and puts them out of the church** (v. 10). **Demetrius** (v. 12), on the other hand, **received a good testimony** (v. 12), and presumably is one of those **fellow workers for the truth ... worthy of God** (vv. 8, 6).

Revelation of John

The Book of Revelation was addressed **to** (Christ's) **servants ...** (in) **the churches that are in Asia** (Revelation 1.1, 4). It was written to their life setting and mine, particularly as I identify with their situation. Believers of all ages have much in common and this takes some of the mystery out of this *unveiling.* Understanding apocalyptic imagery is not an exact science. Still, **blessed are those who hear and who keep what is written** (v. 3). Fidelity to all I read is my goal.

The Book of Revelation has a blend of tenses. Not a problem for **the Alpha and Omega ... first and last** (1.8, 17); not a problem for me. It opens with the future–**things that must soon take place** (v. 1) and quickly shifts to present realities. He is **the ruler of the kings on earth** (v. 5). He **loves us and has freed us from sins ... and made us a kingdom** (vv. 5, 6). Absorbing this is a must, especially for those **in ... tribulation** (v. 9).

All eyes on the Revelator, **Jesus Christ ... the word of God ... the faithful witness, the firstborn from the dead and the ruler of kings ... to him be glory and dominion forever and ever** (Revelation 1.1, 2, 4, 6). He is **the Alpha and Omega ... the Almighty** (v. 8). Much more description to come in vv. 13-16. At my core I need more of God–more Christology. I bring the knowledge of God to my day, my challenges and my needs.

Churches need encouragement and exhortation and in Revelation 1 - 3 there is plenty of both. **I saw ... in the midst of the lampstands,** (i.e. churches - cf. 1.20), **... one like the son of man** (Revelation 1.12). Christ is with us (unless we are an apostate mess)! We believe in his presence and live accordingly. It is real. Then come the exhortations. The Ephesians were **toil**(ing) **and enduring** (2.2, 3) but they were grunting through their obedience without **the love ...** (they) **had at first** (2.4). From love must come **the works** (2.5).

What makes for a good church? **works ... toil ... patient endurance ... not bear**(ing) **with those who are evil ... not grow**(ing) **weary** (Revelation 2.2, 3; cf. v. 6). As for their lack of **love** (v. 4), the call is to **repent** (v. 5). Evidently we can repent from *an emotion!* Feelings do not rule. I do not wait for my flat, unambitious (possibly negative) spirit to change. I respond to revelation!

Trouble was normal in Smyrna: **I know your tribulation ... you will have tribulation ... you are about to suffer** (Revelation 2.9, 10)–a reality more universal than we care to accept. Similarly, with the anticipation **the devil is about to throw some of you into prison** (v. 10). Satan gets credit for what people in power do! **faithful unto death** (v. 10) is our response.

Churches expect opposition. Sardis and Laodicea were imploding under the weight of their own sin but the other 5 churches had formidable opponents: **Nicolaitans** (Revelation 2.6, 15), **a synagogue of Satan** (2.9; 3.9), **Satan's throne** (2.13), and **Jezebel** (2.20). Licentiousness, empty profession, idolatry and other bad teaching infiltrate the church. Hence, the call to be vigilant lest he (Christ) come and **remove ...** (the) **lampstand** (2.5).

you dwell, where Satan's throne is ... where Satan dwells (Revelation 2.13)–a truly difficult environment. They did not choose it. They did not cause it. It is simply their placement from a sovereign God. Along with an encouragement–**you did not deny my name** (v. 13), comes the disclosure of the bad **teaching** (v. 14) and bad behavior (v. 14) tolerated in their midst. *I* will be **the one who conquers** (v. 17). An intolerant God will come to judge (v. 16)!

Repeated themes: (1) **the one who conquers**–7x in Revelation 2&3. Believers are expected to **conquer.** Not survive ... attend ... affirm ... but **conquer**! Explanation: It has much to do with (2) **works** (2.1, 19; 3.1, 8, 15)–**toil ... love and faith and service and patient endurance** (2.2, 19, cf. 2.13; 3.10). Passivity and sloth are not accepted. (3) God sees! **I know** (7x). (4) 7x he promises reward.

(5) Churches have a unique blend of strengths *and impurities,* e.g., **those who call themselves apostles ... abandoned the loved ... had at first ... the teaching of Balaam** (and) **of the Nicolaitans ... sexual immorality... a reputation for being alive but ... are dead ... neither hot nor cold** (Revelation 2.1, 4, 14, 15, 20; 3.1, 15). We do inventory and address the needs, knowing that if we don't, God will (2.5, 16, 22; 3.3, 9, 19)!

Promise is a wonderful motivator. God's promises require faith to see and receive. He is emphatic: **I will give** (Revelation 2.10, 17, 28); **I will confess his name** (3.5); **I will** make (3.12); **I will grant** (3.21). For eyes of faith to see and receive the **life** (2.10), the pardon (2.17; 3.5), the reward (3.12), and the overall presence of God (2.26-28; 3.12)!

God's throne continues to appear in John's vision (Revelation 3.21; cf. 1.4). Once again John is taken to **a throne ... with one seated on the throne** (4.2). Throne speaks of *authority* in 2.13, to be reclaimed by God from the usurping Satan. The throne is the center of worship in chapter 4. **the living creatures give glory and honor and thanks to him who is seated on the throne ... fall**(ing) **down before him** (4.9, 10). I live before the throne!

Behold, I stand at the door ... behold, a door (Revelation 3.20; 4.1). A door to what? Not a *what.* It is a door to him. Although this was already made clear in 3.20, Revelation will devote the next 3 chapters to *him,* despite the stated theme, **what must take place** (4.1). Around his **throne** (4.2, 4) is lots of dazzle (4.3-5.8). The **thrones ... elders ... living creatures ... myriads** (4.4, 8; 5.8, 11) serve as the entourage to the one who is **Worthy ... Lion ... Lamb** (4.11; 5.9, 5, 6)!

I saw ... a scroll (Revelation 5.1)–the most prominent scroll in the Bible. Its opening will be strung out for several chapters. We are not exactly told the contents but that is not the main point. **Who is worthy to open the scroll ... ?** (v. 2). Jesus! Jesus is described as **the Lion ... the Root ... a Lamb standing, as though it had been slain, with seven horns and seven eyes** (vv. 5, 6). He is the majestic, royal, and promised Savior with all power and knowledge!

Those who worship the Lamb are holding **golden bowls full of incense, which are the prayers of the saints** (Revelation 5.8). = *I must pray!* My petitions have a long shelf life, secure in the bowl. These prayers rise **before God** and are thrown back down **on the earth** (8.4) = God responds to intercessions! Faith in Jesus transforms prayer *from* the typical expression of worry or superstition *to* participation with the living God in the unfolding of his will!

Jesus **has conquered** (Revelation 5.5). Then **the rider ... (on) a white horse ... came our conquering and to conquer** (6.2) = the battle is over, and not over. The sin problem has been dealt with *but* remains an issue. There was a judgment on the cross *and* one to come. *God* is responsible for **the seven seals** (6.1), and sends a **rider ... to take peace from the earth** (6.2). For those **who had been slain for the Word of God** there will be justice (6.9, 10).

With the opening of the sixth seal came revelation of **the great day of ... wrath** (Revelation 6.17), i.e. Judgment Day, then a shift: John heard from an angel about 144,000 **from every tribe of the sons of Israel** (7.4), probably the church, already identified as priests (cf. 1.6; 5.10). This report is overshadowed by what John saw: **a great multitude ... before the throne ... clothed in white ... crying out** (vv. 9, 10), followed by great worship from mankind and angels alike!

from every nation, from all tribes and people and languages (Revelation 7.9)–**the ones coming out of the great tribulation** (v. 14) are those **before the throne of God, and serve him day and night in the temple** (v. 15). *Which* great tribulation? Probably from **the great day** (see 6.17), yet *not* excluding other troubles in the church (see 1.9), as in Smyrna (see 2.9) and Thyatira (see 2.22). More important than the identity of the tribulation saints is *what* they all do. Read on.

This is heaven: **the Lamb is in the midst of the throne will be their shepherd, and he will guide them to springs of living water, and God will wipe away every tear** (Revelation 7.17). The Savior / the shepherd is still shepherding. Whatever it is I am doing, I am guided. Life is overflowing. Reward comes in the form of comfort and completion. Heaven is as active and dynamic as God!

Now the seven angels who had the seven trumpets prepared to blow them (Revelation 8.6). Which seven angels? The seven angels associated with and looking after the church (cf. 1.20). Here the church, through angels, is participating in judgment as foretold (see 1 Corinthians 6.2). The seven trumpets revelation is more descriptive than the *seven seals,* to be followed by **seven thunders** (10.3) and **three woes** (9.12), like a dream that rolls along without end. This section does end at 11.19.

Revelation 8.6-11.19 features physical destruction and demonic warfare. Of surprise to me, **the rest of mankind who were not killed by these plagues did not repent of the works of their hands nor give up worshiping demons and idols** (Revelation 9.20). These sinners are *going down with the ship.* Or, a better analogy *fighting to the last man.* Fighting God! Anything but repent. It is sick! And sad.

An angel releases/introduces another angel who reveals a horrific implosion and collapse for those **who do not have** the seal of God (Revelation 9.4). They are *not* **the servants of our God** (7.3). There is nothing to indicate they knew their leader was **Apollyon** (9.11). Remember, evil's forte is deception! Now there is **torment … like the torment of a scorpion** (9.5). Figurative. Symbolic. Not good, with **still** (more) **to come** (9.11, cf. vv. 12-21)! Nevertheless, **they did not repent** (9.20, 21).

a little scroll (Revelation 10.2; cf. vv.2-10) is introduced. Revelation has big books/scrolls and little books/scrolls–same Greek root: biblios. The big book/scroll features the names of the saved (3.5; 20.15; 22.19); the little book/scroll features the details of judgment (10.9, 10). (Again, note the balance of love and righteousness.) Why is it little? **the mighty angel** (with a) **face like the sun … like a lion roaring** (10.1) dispatches judgment as if working off a notepad. A much bigger deal for John (10.10)!

measure the temple … not the court outside he temple, leave that out (Revelation 11.1, 2). **measure** signals great care and attention. Not everything receives it. **the court outside the temple** is part of the temple complex but **it is given over to the nations** (v. 2). The principle here for the church is profound: those who play it safe, who have it their way, who tolerate idolatry and the way of self, *God will let go.* His love for and protection of the temple is great. Those on the periphery he **leave**(s) **… out** (v. 2)!

Q. Why was God so tough on **Sodom and Egypt** (Revelation 11.8)? A. To leave a foreboding warning to what will fall upon the whole world. This **sixth angel** (9.13) is mighty descriptive regarding the destruction to come. Here's the point: the world passes through the holy "meat grinder" and it is then revealed **The kingdom of the world has become the kingdom of our Lord and of his Christ, and he shall reign** (11.15)! **wrath** then **reign** (11.18).

Revelation 10.8-11.13 is a tribute to the great apocalyptic prophets. Familiarity with them precedes my understanding of this section. While details may be speculative, the large themes are clear. John, like Ezekiel, eats a **the little scroll** (10.9). The **bitter** (10.10) taste signals the coming judgment. The **two prophets** (11.10), as affirmed by Zechariah in his day, confirm the prophecy. The **1260 days** (11.3) validate Daniel's description of the end.

Revelation 11-13 includes familiar themes: God's **two witnesses … prophesy** (Revelation 11.3) with authority (11.6), for which **the beast** (11.7) kills them and with much support. These **two prophets had been a torment to those who dwell on earth** (11.10). **the nations raged** (v. 18). **the deceiver** (12.7; cf. 13.14) now takes his turn at wielding **great authority** (13.2, 5; cf. 13.12-14). He establishes his own **mark** (13.16, 17; see 7.3; 14.1). For all this he will fall hard!

Perhaps the last doctrine for Christians to accept is *glory in judgment.* Almost every part of our culture has a resistance to hell's reality and appeals to a God of love. Love and righteousness meet in the **Lord God Almighty** (Revelation 11.16). He is the God of **great power** (v. 17) and appropriately sends **wrath …** (to) **the nations** (that) **raged … The time for the dead to be judged and for rewarding … servants … who fear your name** (v. 18) has come. He **destroy**(s) **… the destroyers** (v. 18).

See *the present* in Revelation 12 more than a *future* event. Both ways, there are clear truths from this figurative section: (1) The spiritual warfare is great. Though **the dragon ... was defeated** (Revelation 12.7, 8), he remains **deceiver of the whole world** (v. 9) and **accuser of our brothers ... day and night** (v. 10). No fear. He has **been conquered by the blood of the Lamb and by the word of their testimony** (v. 11). The believer's authority!

(2) Believers are known for putting Christ first. The **brothers** (Revelation 12.10) are those who **loved not their lives even unto death ... those who keep the commandments of God and hold to the testimony of Jesus** (vv. 11, 17)–the central motivation for all martyrs. For them and everyone else, evidences of a commitment to Jesus must be obvious. We find our life in obedience–and love it!

This battle has always been. It was true at the incarnation, which Revelation 12.1-6 describes apocalyptically. It was true after the incarnation (12.13)–**the dragon became furious with the woman** (12.17). It is true today and will be true at the end. All who **keep the commandments of God and hold to the testimony of Jesus** (12.17) will be in the crosshairs of evil which **make**(s) **war on the saints ... to conquer them** (13.7; cf. 12.17). Receive this as **a call for ... endurance and faith** (13.10; cf. 14.12).

Chapters 13 & 14 of Revelation contrast evil and virtue. Chapter 13: Evil. Two beasts and a dragon picture a future conflict (with additional counterparts throughout history). Characteristics: (1) central and **great authority** (v. 2); (2) a comeback from the dead (vv. 3, 12); (3) **the whole earth** marveled as they followed (v. 3); (4) **war on the saints** (v. 7); (5) **great signs** (v. 13); (6) idolatry (v. 14).

Evil is formidable, but loses to **the sounds of harpists** (Revelation 14.2) and music sung by the redeemed! Then comes the testimony of **the eternal gospel ... proclaim**(ed) ... **to every nation and tribe and language and people** (v. 6). Then the pronouncement, **Fallen, fallen is Babylon the Great** (v. 8). Then some of the terms of judgment: (1) for the faithful **rest from their labors** (v. 13). (2) **Anyone ...** (who) **worships the beast ... he will torment ... and they have no rest, night or day** (vv. 9-11).

Everyone has a **mark on the right hand or the forehead** (Revelation 13.16). For some it is **the name of the beast** (13.17) and for others the name of **the Lamb ... and his Father** (14.1). Minimally, this means everyone knows where everyone stands. I want to be among those with **a call for the endurance and faith** (13.10), with whom **no lie was found** (14.5), **who keep the commandments of God and their faith in Jesus** (14.12).

Revelation 14 describes (1) exemplary believers, referred to here as **first fruits** (v. 4). They have **not defile**(ed) **themselves** and have **follow**(ed) **the lamb** (v. 4) **blameless** (v. 5), obedient and faithful (v. 12)! Perhaps this explains why **they were singing** (v. 3). Wholly committed. Unto death (v. 13). (2) The counterpart of the first fruits are the **grapes ... for the great winepress of the wrath of God** (vv. 18, 19). The judgment section (vv. 8-20) receives more attention.

Acknowledging recapitulation, i.e. the end and judgment being described different ways and not as a repeated series of events, sure makes for easier reading in Revelation 14-18. **a sea of glass mingled with fire** (15.2) signals two concurrent themes. There is **wrath** (Revelation 14.19), **wrath** (15.7) and more **wrath** (16.10). There is accompanying worship (15.3, 4; 16. 5, 6) centering on God's **deeds ... name ...hol**(iness) **...just**(ice) (15.3, 4; 16.7).

a sea of glass mingled with fire ... a sea of glass with harps (Revelation 15.1, 2). **And they sing the song of Moses ... and the song of the Lamb** (v. 3). The judgment about to be pronounced (vv. 3, 4) comes from the totality of God's revelation *and* nature *and* includes his love and grace. Judgment is the inevitable and logical outcome of transgression, dismissed by sinners, because sinners are blind (cf. 3.17).

In the first 5 **bowls of wrath** (Revelation 16.1; cf. 1-11) mankind loses the common grace support system, so easily taken for granted. Infections do not heal, the water is bad and the weather is severe, nonetheless, **they did not repent of their deeds** (v. 11). Then the demonic nature of the world is exposed (vv. 13, 14). The defeat in a battle **called Armageddon** (v. 16) has no military description here. The sentence is pronounced, **It is done** (v. 17).

We are born in sin (Psalm 51.5) and unless this is checked, we degenerate. Revelation16 & 17 reveals mankind at its worse. (1) Intolerance: **they shed the blood of the saints and prophets** (16.6). (2) Pride: **They did not repent** (16.9, 11). (3) Hatred for God: They **cursed the God of heaven** (16.11).

Creation deniers and atheists end up cursing the God they do not believe in! They never understand the reason for **pain and sores** (16.10) and still (4) **make war** (17. 14).

The earliest events recorded in the Bible are (1) the spiritual rebellion (Isaiah 14; Ezekiel 28) and (2) creation (Genesis 1). The judgment of Revelation 16 &17 revisits. (1) **the beast ... the false prophet ... unclean spirits** (16.13, 14) all receive a detailed judgment (through chapter 22). (2) The unacknowledged Creator uses **the sea** (16.3), **the rivers** (16.4), **the sun** (16.8), **thunder and a great earthquake** (16.18) and **mountains** (16.20) in judgment. The end corresponds with the beginning!

It is done for **Babylon the great** (Revelation 16.17, 19). Nonetheless, chapters 17 &18 will further describe her judgment. Lots of images: she is the **great prostitute seated on many waters ... a woman sitting on a scarlet beast ...** (with) **seven heads and ten horns** (17.1, 3). The latter clearly refers to Rome (17.9); the former clearly refers to more than Rome (17.15, 18; 18.9). The seen and unseen stronghold of evil, with its beloved economy (18.7-19), will be **thrown down with violence and will be found no more** (18.21).

I understand Babylon to be the **kingdom ... plunged into darkness ...** (that) **cursed God ...** (and) **did not repent ...** (known for) **sexual immorality ... drunk with the blood of the saints ... a dwelling place of demons ... rich from the power of her luxurious living** (Revelation 16.10; 17.2, 6; 18.2, 3; cf. vv. 11-19). The **voice from heaven** (18.4) explains that the punishment fits the crime (18.4-8). **his judgments are true and just** (19.1).

I am to be wary of culture and the government it creates. Not fearful and condemning, or withdrawing from, just suspicious. **Babylon ... has become a dwelling place of demons** (Revelation 18.1). **Come out of her, my people ... her sins are heaped high as heaven ... weep and wail over her** (vv. 3, 5, 9). The house of cards comes falling down. **The merchants ... weep and mourn ... the fruit for which your soul longed is gone from you** (vv. 11, 14). **The great city ... has been laid waste ... found no more** (vv. 15, 17, 21). The old normal is gone!

In Revelation 19 **he has judged the great prostitute** (v. 2). (The defeat of Satan comes in chapter 20!) This revelation is couched in worship! (1) There is much praise as the wages of sin are paid. **Hallelujah ... glory ... praise to our God** (vv. 1, 5). **the twenty four elders and the four living creatures** (and I - v. 10) **fell down and worshiped God** (v. 4). (2) Then the attention shifts to the victor–**the Lamb ... Faithful and True ... The Word of God** (vv. 9, 11, 13).

As in chapter 1, Revelation 19.11-16 gives an apocalyptic description of Jesus. (1) He is **Faithful and True** (v. 11). (2) **in righteousness he judges and makes war** (v. 11). (3) His appearance and character are beyond human grasping (v. 12), yet I am to remember the **blood** (v. 13) and priestly garments (v. 14). (4) He is **The Word of God** (v. 13) and speaks with **a sharp sword** (v. 15; cf. Hebrews 4.12). (5) **he will rule** (v. 15) as **King of kings and Lord of lords** (v. 16).

Revelation, like Psalms, is a lyrical treasure chest for Christian music. A sampler: **Holy, holy, holy is the Lord God Almighty** (Revelation 4.8); **Worthy are you, our Lord and** our God (4.11); **Salvation belongs to our God** (7.10); **We give thanks to you, Lord God Almighty** (11.17); **Great and amazing are your deeds** (15.3); **Hallelujah!** (19.1, 6); **Praise our God ... you who fear him** (19.5).

Revelation is about future events, worship, spiritual warfare, heaven ... and judgment, the theme presented once again in Revelation 19.17 - 20.15. Judgment is the reason for **Hallelujah!** (19.1, 3). Judgment is presented again in 21.8 and 22.15, just when I think we have moved on. Evil is defeated multiple times in chapters 12-21. In the end, evil and those **who had** (been) **deceived ... will be tormented ... forever and ever** (20.10).

The angels of Revelation have not yet finished their description of the battle, which appeared to be finished back in 6.17. The martyrs, the mark and final judgment are once again in view (20.3, 4, 10, 15) but there are new details: **the thousand years ... Gog and Magog ... a great white throne ... the second death** (20.4, 8, 11, 14). No need for confusion at this point. Too much has already been revealed and is clear.

Evil is a pesky opponent that keeps returning. It should be long gone by Revelation 20.7 but it is not. An impenitent **Satan** (v. 2) emerges after 1000 years in a **pit ... to deceive the nations that are at the four corners of the earth** (Revelation 20.3, 8). Millennial saints must beware of deception. Temptation is never passe. We need lots of help–lots of light to overcome the expert deceiver.

The finish line is in sight! Revelation 21 and 22 brings completion to some New Testament themes: (1) **the dwelling place of God is with man** (21.3). See Ephesians 2.22. (2) **To the one who is thirsty I will give from the spring of water** (21.6). See John 7.37, 38. (3) **conquerors will have this heritage** (21.7). See Romans 8.37. (4) **I will show you the Bride** (21.9). See John 3.29. (5) **he ... showed me the holy city** (21.9, 10). See Hebrews 13.14. (6) **They will see his face** (22.4). See John 1.18.

In Revelation 21 &22 **the sea is no more ... death shall be no more ... mourning ... crying ... pain ... former things have passed away** (21.1, 4). Also **the temple ... sun ... moon ... night** (22.22, 23, 25). In its place, **a new heaven and a new earth** (21.1) introduced with two images: (1) **the holy city** (21.2) noted for its **radiance like a rare jewel** (21.11; cf. vv. 17-21) and its 3 dimensional size (21.16, 17). It is created for **the thirsty ... (and) conquerors** (21.6, 7)!

(2) the angel then directs to **the middle of the street of the city ... the river of the water of life ... flowing from the throne ... the tree of life** (Revelation 22.1, 2; cf. Genesis 3.2) where is found **the throne of God and of the Lamb ... They will see his face** (22.3, 4). Relationship with God, who is relational to the core, is restored! A wonderful ending to the book and to the Bible, the importance of which is underscored in 22.6-21.

These words are trustworthy and true (Revelation 22.6). keep the words of this book (v. 9; cf. 18.19). Yes, the reference is to the book of Revelation but Revelation refers to and validates book after book, Old Testament and New, hence, it is safe to say the whole Bible is here affirmed. The word of God is central for all who **worship God** (v. 9) and have a **share in the tree of life** (v. 19). **Amen. Come, Lord Jesus!** (v. 20).

Made in the USA
Columbia, SC
21 April 2018